酒

FACTS • TIPS • LORE • LIBATION

saké

pure + simple

Griffith Frost

John Gauntner

Stone Bridge Press • Berkeley, California

Published by

Stone Bridge
Press
P.O. Box
8208
Berkeley
CA 94707

tel 510-524-8732
sbp@stonebridge.com
www.stonebridge.com

Enjoy saké sensibly and responsibly!

The publisher would like to acknowledge with gratitude the assistance
of the many breweries and establishments mentioned in this book.
Corrections and updates would be greatly appreciated. Please e-mail
correspondence to sbp@stonebridge.com.

Text © 1999 International Saké Institute. Forest Grove, Oregon.
Line drawings © 1999 L. J. C. Shimoda.
Front cover design and illustration by Karen Marquardt.
Back cover and text design by L. J. C. Shimoda.

10   9   8   7   6   5   4   3   2   1
2003   2002   2001   2000   1999

LIBRARY OF CONGRESS CATALOGING-IN-PUBLICATION DATA
Frost, Griffth.
Saké, pure + simple: facts, tips, lore, libation /
Griffith Frost, John Gauntner.
p.   cm.
Includes bibliographical references and index.
ISBN 1-880656-37-X
1. Rice wines. I. Gauntner, John, II. Title.
III. Title: Saké, pure and simple.
TP579.F76   1999
641.2'3—dc21   99-381883
CIP

CONTENTS

Saké Moments
Friends recall occasions when saké made the difference

Saké Slugfests
The authors duke it out for saké supremacy!

INTRODUCTION

Saké, often called the "Drink of the Gods" by the Japanese, is a beverage created from rice, water, *koji-kin* (an enzyme), and yeast, usually with an alcohol content of around 15%, about that of wine. Saké is brewed like a beer, but it is served like a wine. Premium saké is usually served slightly chilled, while lower grades of saké are often served warm. Saké is best enjoyed with lightly prepared fish, chicken, pork, vegetarian, and Asian cuisine . . .

WHAT MAKES SAKÉ SO GOOD?

In its pure form, saké is one of the most natural beverages on earth. It contains only rice, water, yeast, and *koji-kin* (an enzyme).

Saké has a lower acidity than wine.

Wine has one fermentation agent, yeast. But saké uses yeast *and koji-kin* to produce a beverage that is 20% alcohol. Water is added to dilute the alcohol content down to 15%, just a bit higher than that of wine.

Saké, unlike wine, contains no sulfites (and 10% of Americans are allergic to sulfites!).

Premium saké, compared to wine, is virtually hangover free.

Saké promotes a healthy eating style, since saké is best served with fresh or lightly prepared foods.

In Japan, studies show that people who enjoy saké daily strengthen their cardiovascular system without wine's characteristic "sour stomach."

Saké has 400 flavor components; wine has 200.

Saké, compared to wine, is more subtle and delicate, which enhances saké's ability to serve as a social catalyst promoting wonderful relationships.

And there is a legend, subscribed to by many, that saké is an aphrodisiac . . . but some of the mysteries of saké are better left unrevealed!

We Were in a Saké Bar and . . .

The small, twelve-tatami-mat saké bar, located in a house, secreted down a back alley of a residential neighborhood of Tokyo, is known only to the saké cognoscenti. To be admitted to this saké bar, you need to be introduced by one of its regular patrons.

In this saké bar, there are over two hundred different kinds of saké available by the glass, all of them stored in refrigerated cases around the room. Many of the sakés are procured from small breweries that annually make only two bottles available to each of their favorite saké bars, who must often order years in advance.

Since 1988 I had made this saké bar a "must visit" place each time I visited Tokyo. In 1994, I was surprised to see, for the first time, another American there, my coauthor, John Gauntner. Over many wonderful glasses of premium saké, we found we had a common mission: to reveal the mysteries of the saké world so that Americans could enjoy and understand the very best of this amazing and delicious beverage.

At the time, saké was a mysterious liquid produced by secretive Japanese saké breweries, with the finest sakés being available only to those few "in the know."

Even the saké brewed in the U.S. was being sold in bottles with no explanation about what saké was or how it should be drunk. And, horror of horrors, most of the saké sold in America was being served piping hot—destroyed!—out of saké machines in Japanese restaurants. Premium chilled saké was a rarity. And books about saké, the few that were available in English, were focused on explanations about saké in Japan.

But times are changing, and many more Americans are aware of premium saké and are enjoying it in restaurants that know how to serve it. And with this book, my coauthor, John, and I intend to make sure this trend continues. Our backgrounds put us in a unique position to do the job. After living in Japan for thirteen years, I established in Forest Grove, Oregon, what would become the first American-owned saké brewery in the world. SakéOne (which started life as the Japan America Beverage Company) today imports saké from Japan and brews—in the U.S.—a complete line of premium sakés. John, an American, has lived in Tokyo for ten years and is now recognized as America's leading saké expert.

Over the past five years, systematically, in Japanese and English, we gathered information about the saké world from sources in Japan and North America. Much of the information was contradictory. We identified and resolved each of these contradictions.

The result is *Saké: Pure + Simple*. We expect our book to be just the beginning of our efforts to educate Americans about the joys of premium saké. At the back of the book you'll find blank tasting charts, plus information resources to help you stay abreast of the latest developments in the world of saké.

We look forward to corresponding with you, and with the ever-growing number of fellow American saké enthusiasts.

Kanpai!

GRIF FROST
FOREST GROVE, OREGON

Write to Grif Frost and John Gauntner at sakeexperts@sakes.com.

Saké in the United States

One out of every five glasses of wine consumed in the world is saké. In the United States, one out of every hundred glasses of wine is saké. U.S. saké consumption from 1990 to 1995 doubled in size, and from 1996 to 1998 it doubled again. We think saké consumption in the United States may triple by the end of the year 2000.

Why?

One reason is increased supply. There are now seven saké breweries that have collectively invested over $200 million in brewery facilities in California, Colorado, and Oregon. Three major Japanese saké breweries have U.S. sales offices. Plus, over a hundred Japanese saké breweries are exporting their brands to the U.S. The number of saké labels regularly available in the U.S., we estimate, increased from 50 in 1990 to over 350 in 1999.

In addition, saké is moving out of purely Japanese restaurants and into American restaurants eager to experiment with new foods and drinks. Saké has leapt out of the strictly Asian markets and is now sold in virtually every supermarket with a fine wine section. There are today over a hundred non-Japanese-owned saké bars in the United States, up from zero in 1990.

To put it simply: more quality saké is available in the United States than ever before, and this is leading more and more Americans to discover and to enjoy this luscious brew.

Another reason behind increased saké consumption is education. American consumers are becoming aware of the benefits of enjoying pure and natural saké—little to no hangover, no sulfites, half the acidity of wine—the perfect enhancement to a healthy lifestyle.

While enjoying a Big Mac at a McDonalds in Japan, a young Japanese girl was recently overheard asking her father, "Daddy, are there McDonalds in America?" Perhaps at some dinner table in the year 2010 an American child will ask her parents, who are enjoying a glass of premium saké, "Mom and Dad, do Japanese drink saké?"

A friend writes: One of my first introductions to cold saké was in Japan during cherry blossom time. I was there on a high-level business trip and one evening was taken to one of the best geisha houses in Tokyo. My saké arrived in the traditional wooden box with three cherry blossom petals floating on the surface. This, my host explained, was to give me the impression that I was out in a beautiful park admiring the blossoming cherry trees and the wind had blown the blossoms into my saké. My wife was back in America, but I was able to have a wonderful image of exactly what it would have been like had the two of us been able to share a picnic under a cherry tree on a windy afternoon. It was a sad, but beautiful picture.

KANPAI!

At weddings, dinner parties, and informal get-togethers, the word *kan-pai* is used as the standard Japanese toast.

It is written with two *kanji* characters: "dry" + "cup." The meaning is obvious: let's drain our glasses in friendship!

"dry" + *"cup"*

LET'S TALK SAKÉ!

You don't have to know how to speak Japanese to enjoy saké. And we promise that this book is written in simple English. But there are a number of basic Japanese saké terms you should know if you're going to seriously get into saké. ☞ For the names of different types of saké and brewing stages, see the detailed explanations on pages 22–40. ☞ For tasting terms, see pages 96–97. Here are a few other common saké terms used in this book or among saké aficionados.

- *kura*: saké brewery
- *toji*: chief brewer; sakémaster
- *-shu*: written with the same kanji as the word "saké," *-shu* is a suffix meaning "wine" or "wine-like beverage"; the word "Junmai-shu" simply means "saké made in the Junmai [literally, 'pure rice'] style"; frequently heard is "Nihonshu," literally, "Japanese wine," which is a generic term for any Japanese saké

-shu or "saké"

  - *hiyazake:* saké served at room temperature or lightly chilled; another word for chilled sake is *reishu*
  - *kanzake*: saké that is served warm

Usually Japanese words aren't pluralized (says our editor), but in this book we're treating "saké/sakés" just like an English word (except for that little accent on the e for pronunciation) because that's probably the best way to get people to start thinking of saké as a universal beverage.

Saké Culture

HISTORY, RITUAL, BUSINESS

A Brief History of Saké

Saké is believed to have originated in China, in the Yangtze River Valley, as long ago as 4800 B.C. Today there are over 1,800 saké kura (breweries) making more than 40,000 types of saké. In the United States, seven modern saké kura produce over 100 types of sakés to complement the 250+ sakés being imported from Japan.

After its early evolution in China, saké made its way into Japan soon (not surprisingly) after wet rice cultivation was begun in the third century B.C. Around A.D. 689, an imperial brewing department was set up by the Japanese court, and saké brewing became a bit more refined. Soon saké started to be brewed in temples and shrines, endowed as they were with copious amounts of land, water, rice, and thirsty monks. Progress was slow, and saké did not take the form it has today for another four hundred years.

Technology was developed piece by piece but was not always immediately implemented. Knowledge about water, rice handling, sanitation, and chemistry gradually began to supplant experience. By the end of the 19th century, making saké had come to be an industrial process that could consistently produce a clean and palatable beverage.

Just after the turn of the 20th century, innovations in such areas as rice milling technology, pure yeast cultures, chemical analysis, sanitation, and glass bottles helped boost the grade of saké overall. The Ministry of Finance even set up a saké research center (after all, better saké means more taxes).

This scientific tendency has accelerated over the last twenty years. There are new yeasts isolated for very specific characteristics, and new rice types as well. Water can be chemically adjusted if necessary. Modern measuring equipment, plumbing, and climate-control technology allow close to ideal conditions to be reproduced at will, removing guesswork and error. Although human experience and intuition are still indispensable in saké brewing, technology has done its share to make saké today significantly better than ever.

DRINK OF THE GODS

Saké has long been linked to the ancient indigenous religion of Japan, Shinto. The main saké-brewing patron deity is the god of the Matsuo Taisha shrine at the foot of Mount Arashi in Kyoto, and he is generally referred to by name as Matsuo-sama. Small shrines dedicated to Matsuo-sama and other gods are often found inside breweries. In ordinary homes are *kamidana*, or "god shelves," where devotions are paid to both deceased relatives and the protecting household gods. It is worth noting that each day the ancestors are served water—while the gods are served saké.

An interesting ritual called *o-miki* is performed at a shrine and involves a Shinto priest taking a small taste of saké from a white porcelain cup as he stands before the altar. This is a sign of communion with the godly powers that be and usually expresses a petition for a dollop of good fortune. *O-miki* is more than just tossing one back with the gods. By imbibing a small portion of saké in this way, and in this setting and context, it is believed that you take a bit of the god-force into yourself, becoming somehow at one with the gods.

Saké Associations

Saké associations are usually made up of saké breweries, resellers, and consumers who are interested in educating people about saké and hence increasing the size of the industry. In Japan there are three main associations of saké breweries: Nihon Meimon Shukai (Japan Prestige Saké Association), Nihon-san Seishu Yushutsu Kiko (Saké Service Institute), and Nihonshu Yushutsu Kyokai (Saké Export Association). All three associations are actively involved in promoting the charms and wonders of Nihonshu (saké, that is) around the world. Other organizations, like Nihon Ginjoshu Kyokai (Japan Ginjo Saké Organization) and Junsui Nihonshu Kyokai (Pure Saké Organization), focus their activities more on what's happening in Japan. There is also a central organization for all brewers throughout Japan known as Nihonshuzo Kumiai Chuokai (Japan Central Brewer's Union).

In the United States are two native-born saké associations. The Saké Association of America (SAA) is composed of representatives of the seven U.S. saké breweries and three large Japanese saké breweries that export to Japan. The Saké Resource Center (SRC) of the International Saké Institute (ISI) was founded by American saké enthusiasts and is dedicated to promoting the enjoyment of saké worldwide. See the listings at the back of this book for contact information, particularly if you'd like to become a saké supporter.

Saké and Distribution

How does saké get from the brewery to you? If brewed in Japan, the saké is generally sold to a wholesaler, who then sells to an exporter, who sells to a U.S. importer, who sells to a U.S. sole agent, who sells to a wholesaler, who sells to your favorite restaurant or retailer, who sells to you. Saké brewed in the U.S. is generally shipped direct from the brewery to the distributor to your local saké bar or saké shop. This is why U.S.-brewed saké is likely to be fresher than imported saké as

SAKÉ: NO HANGOVER?

Premium saké, even when one may overindulge, is nearly hangover free. Why? Congeners, thought to cause hangovers, are generated from the impurities in an alcoholic beverage. The main source of congeners in saké are the proteins and fatty acids in the outside portion of the rice kernel. Since premium saké uses rice milled down to less than 70% of the original kernel size, most of these impurities are eliminated. As they say in Japan: You know good saké the next morning.

well as less expensive. Why is it important that you know this? Because not all shops, dealers, and distributors outside Japan are aware of how time-sensitive saké is on the shelf. To be safe, remember to always check the "freshness" date on the label and buy your saké from a restaurant or retailer who likes saké and knows how to handle it properly. Given proper storage and handling, there's no reason imported saké can't be enjoyed as fresh as its brewer intended.

A friend writes: Yasuda Joshu Dainen Roshi said, "Many Japanese Zen monks lose themselves in saké. The tokkuri flask drinks them dry. They do not know the secret of saké." The monk asked, "What is the secret of saké?" Roshi said, "No no, it is not a big secret, it is a small secret. It fits in each cup of saké. The secret is in the saké. Taste it! Saké tastes like the soil, water, sunlight, the thousand grains of rice that could come from each grain, and the work of harvesting, cleaning, and fermenting by so many workers. This is what saké tastes like and it is why it is so simple and yet so big. If you drink to taste something that is not lonely, you become lonely. If you drink saké to taste happiness but you are not already happy you become unhappy. Drink saké like it is saké and it is *hannya-to* (hot wisdom water)."

Saké and Festive Occasions

Every neighborhood in every city in Japan has its festival. Often these celebrations involve throngs of revelers hoisting a portable shrine called an *omikoshi* on their shoulders and carrying the local deity through the streets. Saké, with its ritual religious connection, is an important part of the occasion, and most active participants consider it the source of their festive vigor.

Until the early 1900s, saké was shipped in and served from cedar barrels. Nowadays, on important occasions—like weddings, opening ceremonies, and anniversaries—special decoratively labeled barrels are broken open with a wooden hammer so that saké can be ladled

SAKÉ AND POETRY

A famous poet in 8th-century China named Li Po (known as Rihaku in Japan) was known to be more than a little fond of the bottle. His motto: "I drink a whole bottle, and pen a hundred poems." He is said to have died by drowning after reaching out for the moon while riding in a boat. Well! Here is a sample of his work:

> *Kakan ikko no sake*
> *Hitorikunde ai shitashimu nashi*
> *Hai wo agete*
> *Meigetsu wo mukae*
> *Kage to taishite*
> *Sannin to naru*

> Amongst the flowers a bottle of saké
> I drink alone, no one to keep me company
> I raise my glass to the moon so bright, and offer a toast
> To the three of us: the moon, my shadow, and me

Rihaku is also the name of a fine saké from Shimane Prefecture. The brewery uses the poet's work in its printed material and labels.

out for a ritual toast. The cedar imparts a crisp, cinnamonlike flavor. Some of the American saké breweries can provide large or small barrels full of fresh saké—an excellent and unforgettable way to commemorate a special event.

SAKÉ SAYINGS

Sake wa hyaku yaku no chô.
"Saké is the best of all [literally, best of 100] medicines."
In English this might be: "A drink a day keeps the doctor away."

Sakenomi jozu wa nagaiki jozu.
"To know how to drink properly is to know longevity."

Sake wa saki ni tomo to nari, ato ni teki ni naru.
"Saké starts out as a friend but can end as an enemy."
Remember the importance of moderation!

Now try this one on your boss. It is from Tokugawa Ieyasu, the famous shogun:

Ippai nomeba yuki ga waki, hito-hataraki suru hodo sei ga deru mono da.
"A good drink fills me with courage, and creates in me the drive to get some work done."

Saké Competitions

In Japan the most important saké competitions are sponsored by the government taxation authorities. This practice is a holdover from the days when the tax on saké depended on its "quality" ranking. Although that system is no longer in use, each year the tax departments throughout Japan hold blind tasting competitions open to all saké breweries in their respective regions. Scores of 1, 2, or 3 are assigned in two rounds, with a score of 1 being the best. A predetermined number of the lowest-scoring (that is, best) sakés are then selected to go on to the national-level competition.

At the national tasting, the same procedure is repeated. In the end, the top-scoring sakés are given a gold prize, and runner-ups receive a silver prize. Although the sakés submitted for such competitions are usually specially brewed batches, and can be a far cry from a kura's everyday saké, such awards are great for bragging rights. "Made by a Gold-Prize-Winning Kura" certainly attracts attention on the shelves.

In the United States, *Wine Enthusiast* magazine sponsors a saké competition with categories for both imported and domestically brewed sakés. In the not-too-distant future ISI's Saké Resource Center will be sponsoring an annual International Saké Celebration, a five-day event open to the trade and the public. There will be saké education courses, saké-judging competitions, and lots of saké and food. See the back of this book for contact information.

How Is Saké Made?

BREWING, INGREDIENTS, VARIETIES

The People

Generally in each brewery—called a kura in Japanese—there is one person known as the toji. The toji is the chief sakémaster. Usually the person with the most experience, until recently the toji was always a man. Not so anymore. Beneath the toji are supporting sakémasters (who actually do most of the labor) known as kurabito, or "people of the kura."

Traditionally the relationship between the toji and the kurabito was a feudal one. The toji and kurabito would often come from distant farms, where they worked and lived in the summer, to brew saké in the winter, as there was no work at home. This practice is gradually changing, however, as more and more local people are hired and regular working hours become commonplace in the breweries. Naturally, the U.S. saké brewing kurabito are not farmers from the countryside but local individuals, usually with advanced science degrees.

Toji

The Method: Art vs. Chemistry

Long ago there were no computers, accurate thermometers, or precise methods for measuring a saké's acidity or exact chemical components. Brewing good saké was a matter of what is called *keiken to kan*, that is, experience and intuition.

Today, saké brewers the world around are blessed with monitoring systems that can accurately report, document, and sometimes adjust practically every saké brewing parameter. Computer screens with graphic displays show every stage of every step.

Many small kura eschew these methods and continue to do things by hand. Yet even in the most modern breweries, all automated processes need to be monitored and are subject to human intervention for subtle adjustments. There is also a point of diminishing returns, beyond which further automation has a detrimental effect on the final product. While the skills of master craftsmen like toji remain indispensable in saké brewing, most of the machines introduced into kura over the last few decades have, in general, made saké production more predictable and economically viable.

Rice and Rice Preparation

One way saké rice differs from eating rice is that the starches—which will later be converted to fermentable sugars—are concentrated in the center of the rice grain. As the outside of the grain is polished away, more and more of the undesirable fat and proteins are removed. How much of the rice remains after polishing—called the *seimaibuai*—depends on the type of saké being brewed; it can range anywhere from 73% to 35%.

The polished rice is then washed to remove all the talc left from the polishing process (a very important step) and soaked to bring the water content of the rice to the desired level. Next, the rice is steamed to a firm consistency, not quite as soft as table rice.

We know of several saké kura in the U.S. who are working with rice research institutes and technologically advanced rice farmers to grow specific strains of saké rice that may one day match the quality of saké rice available to sakémasters in Japan. (There is a rumor that the king of saké rice, Yamada Nishiki, is now being grown in the U.S. from seeds secured in Japan.)

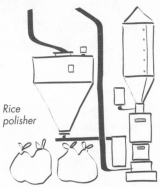

Rice polisher

RICE VARIETIES

Saké rice is not table rice. Although all rice may look the same to the untrained eye, there are major compositional differences between the rice that goes into your sushi and the rice that goes into your saké. Sim-

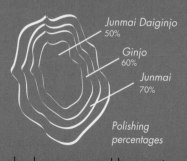

Junmai Daiginjo
50%

Ginjo
60%

Junmai
70%

Polishing
percentages

ply stated, it is a matter of starch, protein, fats, and minerals, among other things.

There are about sixty rice strains designated as *shuzo koteki mai* (saké brewing rice) in Japan. This number changes all the time as new strains are developed through crossbreeding and other techniques; rice strains can also become unusable over time. Some of the more common saké rice strains include such formidable names as Yamada Nishiki, Miyama Nishiki, Gohyakumangoku, and Omachi. Yamada Nishiki in particular, grown in southern Honshu, is well known for its use in high-quality Ginjo sakés.

In the U.S. there is no rice-designating body and there are no types of rice officially designated as saké rice or table rice. This is not to imply that American sakémasters are not aware of the importance of the right rice. They are indeed aware, and are working hard to constantly improve the rice strains available to them and to develop new rice types that will contribute to making better saké.

Water

The quality of the water can affect the quality of the saké. Today, with modern filtration technology, the source of water is not as imporant as it was even as recently as twenty years ago. Both "soft" water and "hard" water are used successfully in brewing saké, but the types of saké that result are vastly different. Often, water is used just as it occurs in its natural state, from a well or spring. Other times, local water that has been doctored is used. Beyond that, there are minerals and elements that promote healthy fermentation, and those that inhibit it. Potassium, magnesium, and phosphoric acid help vigorous yeast propagation and also assist in koji development (see below). Iron and manganese, on the other hand, adversely affect the flavor, aroma, and color of a saké in a relatively short amount of time.

Koji Making

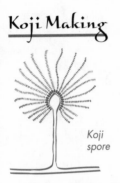

Koji
spore

Part of each batch of steamed rice that goes into a tank of saké is earmarked for koji duty, said to be the heart of the saké brewing process. The koji mold—*koji-kin*, or *Aspergillus oryzae*—is cultivated onto steamed rice that is spread out onto a broad flat tray. This mold eats its way into the rice, and as it does so the enzymes it provides break down the rice's long starch molecules into small sugar molecules that later become food for the yeast cells.

The koji-making process generally takes somewhere between forty-three and forty-eight hours to complete. Extremely dependent on temperature and humidity, it is done in a special room designed to maintain the proper conditions. Koji calls for constant attention and care and is affected by many factors, like the hardness or softness of the water, for example.

Koji
trays

A friend writes: We got off the train somewhere near Nagoya where my friend knew a Shinto priest. We had been invited to a shrine dedication ceremony. We trekked up a slight hill, and there in a bamboo woods was the new-built shrine, smelling of fresh cedar. During the ceremony we received saké in flat cups and sipped in a ritual libation. We knelt for about half an hour as the priest waved the sacred branch and chanted ancient songs. When the ceremony was over, the priest said, "Come." We followed him outside. There he built a small bonfire on the edge of the forest. Taking a length of fresh green bamboo, he sawed off about a foot and carved a hole in the top of one of the joints. Into the section of bamboo he poured fresh saké from a bottle. Then, after applying a hand-fashioned cap, he threw the piece of filled bamboo into the fire. We sat and watched the sunset for a bit, and then the priest removed the bamboo from the fire, pried off the cap, and poured out warm, divine saké into our waiting cups.

When finished, koji looks like rice with a touch of frosting, tastes slightly sweet, and has a fragrance reminiscent of chestnuts. It is always added to the fermenting mixture with plain steamed rice—usually in three separate batches.

Yeast

Before fermentation in a large tank can begin, the toji must create a yeast starter. Known as the moto or shubo, this is a small vatload of water, rice, and koji to which yeast is added and allowed to multiply until there is an extremely high concentration of yeast cells. There are several methods of doing this, but the most common takes about two

At the cellular level, yeast transforms sugar into alcohol

weeks. A small amount of lactic acid is usually added to assist in the growth of yeast cells. After the yeast starter has been properly prepared, it is transferred to a larger tank where more water, rice, and koji can be added to it and the creation of saké can begin.

The choice of yeast at this early stage has a huge effect on the type of saké that results. Different yeast strains have different special qualities. Some create fruitier aromas, others more quiet fragrances; still others work best with particular rice types.

Sandan Shikomi

After the yeast starter is ready, it is transferred to a larger tank. There, steamed rice, koji, and water are added in three separate stages over a period of four days to create the fermentation mixture, called the moromi. Each addition is roughly twice that of the preceding. This three-step process of doubling, redoubling, and again redoubling the mixture is called *sandan shikomi*, or "three-step brewing." It has long

MORE ON YEAST

There are dozens of strains of yeast (*kobo*) used in saké brewing, with new ones being isolated for specific qualities out of hoards of natural yeast cells. There are also "proprietary" yeast strains, discovered by individual kura and used by them alone. It is common to have yeast strains discovered and used extensively within a given prefecture or geographical region.

Until recently, many yeast strains were cultivated and sold in pure form by the National Saké Brewers Association to breweries around the country. These various yeast strains were given numbers corresponding to the order in which they were discovered. Two of the most common yeast strains are Association #7 and Association #9. As many as fifteen are identified and numbered this way, but not all are commonly used.

been practiced in Japan, and what's remarkable is how modern-day science validates the presumably trial-and-error methods of earlier brewers. By adding the ingredients gradually, brewers insure that all the competing factors—the starch from the rice, the sugar-creating enzymes from the koji, the active yeast cells, and the alcohol content— are kept in a careful equilibrium. Too much sugar or not enough, or too high an alcohol concentration in the moromi can kill off the yeast cells, derailing the fermentation and creating an altogether different— and unpleasant—brew. On the second day of *sandan shikomi* nothing is added so that the yeast concentration can recover from its initial dilution. This "skipped" step is called *odori*, "dance," a reference in part to the way the fermentation mixture becomes more lively on its surface.

fermentation

Once all the components have been added in the correct amounts and at the correct time, fermentation is allowed to proceed for anywhere from eighteen to thirty-two days. The moromi at this point resides in a large, open, cylindrical tank. Maintaining it at the optimal temperature is one of the toji's most important jobs. Too warm a temperature risks bacterial infection. Too low might improve the flavor, but slows

Old-style brewing vats

TEN FACTORS IN MAKING GOOD SAKÉ

1. quality of the rice
2. percent the rice is milled
3. how the koji rice is made (machine versus handcrafted)
4. type of yeast
5. type of koji
6. length of aging in temperature-controlled tanks
7. method of filtration
8. quality of the water
9. method of blending
10. skill of the brewing team

the process and may be uneconomical. Because the activity of the moromi produces heat, saké brewing in Japan was traditionally carried out in the winter months. Nowadays, of course, temperature (and every other aspect of the fermentation process) is strictly controlled by machinery. The temperature of the mash varies, but can be as low as 50°F (10°C) for the highly regarded Ginjo type (☞ see page 35).

During fermentation, the koji continues to break down the rice in the vat into sugars (saccharification), while at the same time the yeast is converting these sugars to alcohol and carbon dioxide. Called "multiple parallel fermentation," this is one of the noteworthy characteristics of the saké brewing process. The grapes used in wine making have enough natural sugars to ferment naturally, while in beer making malt is used to change the starch in the grains into sugar prior to the addition of yeast. In saké making, the conversion of rice to sugar and sugar to alcohol occurs simultaneously.

A great foam will rise and fall within the tank. Eventually the life cycle of the yeast expires, and it approaches dormancy. At this point, the alcohol content is about 20%, the highest of all commercially produced beverages.

filtration

Next the saké is separated from the lees (the unfermented rice solids suspended in the liquid). Usually this is done by a large filtering machine with an accordionlike section that fills with air, squeezing the moromi through a series of screen mesh panels. This causes the solids to remain behind, allowing only the saké to pass through.

This type of filtering machine has been around only a few decades, and its predecessor—called a fune—has not been eradicated. In a fune, canvas bags are filled with moromi, laid in a wooden box about the size of a large refrigerator, and pressed with a weight from above. The saké filters out of the canvas bags for collection below.

A more extravagant way of filtration—canvas bags of moromi are simply hung to drip, with no pressure applied—yields some of the most sublime saké available. But for simple economic reasons it is not often used.

After filtration, the saké is pasteurized, stored, bottled, and shipped. Water is added around this stage to dilute the saké to an alcohol level of 15%. The timing, duration, and order of these stages will vary slightly from kura to kura.

Aging

Most saké is aged for about six months before shipping. This allows the rough edge of fresh saké to mellow and blend, rounding out the flavor profile. Some kura, however, insisting that longer aging makes a better product, age their saké a year and a half or more before shipping. Some sakémasters age saké in the glass bottles it will ship in, but most age it in large tanks (identical to the fermentation tanks).

Saké is generally not aged beyond this. If aged under less than ideally controlled conditions, a saké can become unbalanced and cloying. It is always best to consume saké soon after you purchase it. Do not try to age it in storage as you might age fine red wine.

HOMEBREWING SAKÉ

Brewing saké in your home in Japan is illegal (although this does not stop some Japanese "moonshiners" from producing their own prized *doburoku*). Not so in the United States, where many of the estimated two million homebrewers of beer are today experimenting with homebrewing saké. Saké represents a particular challenge to the homebrewer since it uses two fermentation agents, yeast and koji, as opposed to just one—yeast—for beer. Obtaining quality ingredients for homebrewing saké in the U.S. is also difficult. But it's exactly these challenges that appeal to the homebrewer. And who knows, perhaps some of the saké homebrewers' innovations will find their way into the commercial brewery (which is exactly what happened in the beer industry). For more information about homebrewing saké we recommend Fred Eckhardt's book *Saké (U.S.A.)*, which includes detailed recipes.

Bottling

Almost all saké is bottled before shipping. In Japan, saké bottles hold either 1.8 liters or 720 ml, volumes based on a traditional unit for measuring rice. In the U.S., 1.5 liter and 750 ml bottles are the standard sizes (and we would be delighted if someone could tell us why). Corks are not used in saké bottles, since saké is not designed to age, and in any case the cork will discolor the saké. But since exposure to air can be very detrimental to saké stored in bottles, screw-top closures or bar-top closures are used instead. Most larger breweries have an automatic bottling and labeling machine that fills the bottles right from the tanks, pasting on labels and capping bottles in one long process.

The Process: Tying It All Together

Now that the individual steps have been described, here is the gist of how the whole saké brewing process flows from step to step:

- Rice is polished, cleaned, and steamed.

- Koji rice is prepared over a two-day period.

- Steamed rice and cultivated koji are sent to the yeast starter room, and the moto (yeast starter) is prepared over a two-week period.

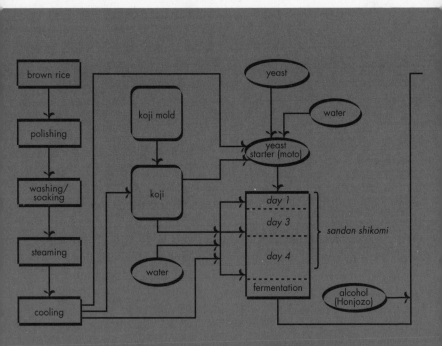

- The moto is transferred to a larger tank, and over a period of four days (on the first, third, and fourth days), rice, water, and the prepared koji are added into the tank, roughly doubling the volume of the mixture each time.

- The moromi (fermenting mixture) runs its course over a period of eighteen to thirty-two days.

- The saké is then ready for filtration, separating the unfermented solids from the clear saké.

- The saké is aged, pasteurized, and blended as required.

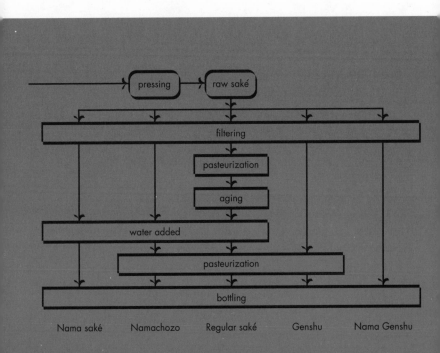

Types of Saké

JUNMAI-SHU

Junmai-shu (or just Junmai, without the suffix -*shu* meaning "wine")
is saké brewed using only rice, water, koji, and yeast. The
name means "pure rice," an indication that no brewer's alcohol has been added to the final product. Often full-bodied
and slightly acidic, Junmai goes well with a wide variety of
foods.

純
米
酒

Tokubetsu ("Special") Junmai is Junmai saké that uses
saké rice that has been milled to 65% or less of its original
size.

HONJOZO-SHU

Honjozo-shu, or just Honjozo, is saké to which a small amount of
brewer's alcohol has been added. This is added near the end
of the fermentation process, just before filtration. Honjozo
saké is generally lighter than Junmai and can be very nice
at room temperature or warmed. The brewer's alcohol has
the bonus effect of bringing out the aroma of the saké quite
nicely.

本
醸
造
酒

Cheap saké will likely have a great deal of added alcohol,
as it is less expensive to produce saké that way. But the
amount of alcohol added to Honjozo is limited to 25% of the
final alcohol total. Honjozo saké is neither contaminated nor
watered down. Some purists will drink only Junmai, but
Honjozo brews have been around for centuries, and many are highly
regarded by top connoisseurs. In the U.S. it is currently not legal to
brew Honjozo or to add distilled alcohol to any saké. Thus, all saké
brewed in the U.S. is by law Junmai saké.

Tokubetsu ("Special") Honjozo, like Tokubetsu Junmai, is Honjozo
that uses saké rice that has been milled to 65% or less of its original
size.

HONJOZO AND THE ATF

Making Honjozo—saké with distilled alcohol added to it (up to 200 liters per metric ton)—is currently illegal in the United States, or so says the Bureau of Alcohol, Tobacco, and Firearms. In addition, imported Honjozo is classified as a distilled alcohol and taxed accordingly upon importation, making it much more expensive than imported Junmai sakés, which contain no brewer's alcohol. Thus, it is very difficult to obtain Honjozo saké in the United States.

But it's not like Honjozo is some completely exotic beverage. In fact, more than 95% of all the saké made in Japan has some alcohol added to it. Honjozo can be wonderful saké indeed, fragrant and light. The added alcohol does increase the alcohol content, but the product is then diluted to bring the alcohol back down to the desired level of 15–16%. Logic would dictate, in the opinion of some, that it should not be subject to fortified or distilled liquor levels of taxation. Efforts are underway to change the laws, but such things take time.

GINJO-SHU

Ginjo-shu, or Ginjo, is saké made with rice polished to the extent that the outer 40% (at least) of each grain has been ground away. This is only the beginning, however, as each step of the Ginjo brewing process is performed with painstaking attention. Care is taken not to crack the rice grains during polishing, fermentation proceeds at lower temperatures and for longer periods, pressing is often done by hand. This extra effort produces a saké that is layered and complex, lighter and more fragrant.

Note that Ginjo comes in both Junmai and Honjozo types. In other words, whether or not brewer's alcohol has been added is an issue *unconnected* to the Ginjo-shu brewing methods. The relative differences between a Junmai Ginjo and Honjozo Ginjo are akin to those between a Junmai and a Honjozo.

DAIGINJO-SHU

Daiginjo-shu, usually referred to as just Daiginjo, is actually a subclassification of Ginjo-shu. At least the outer 50% of each grain of rice has been polished into oblivion, and the various brewing processes are handled with even more care and attention.

Daiginjo is even lighter and more fragrant and fruity than Ginjo. It is not always the best choice and is certainly not everyone's favorite, as it can be too light and delicate. But it does represent the top of the saké line.

大銀醸酒

As with Ginjo, there are both Junmai Daiginjo and Honjozo Daiginjo, depending on whether or not brewer's alcohol has been added to smooth out the final brew.

It should be noted that in Japan, there is no such terminology as Honjo Ginjo or Honjozo Daiginjo. Either a saké qualifies for the Junmai label, having no added brewer's alcohol, or it does not. But we believe such a terminology should exist, and propose that it be adopted, at least in the United States.

FUTSU-SHU

Any saké that does not meet the criteria of the above four classifications is usually called Futsu-shu, which just means "normal saké." The term may simply refer to a saké made with no special ingredients or

A friend writes: My Japanese father-in-law ran a 300-employee construction company in northern Japan. One January, I sat next to him in a large hotel ballroom during the company's New Year's Party. My father-in-law loved saké but that day I noticed he was not drinking at all. After the meal was over I found out why. One by one, each of the 300 employees brought their small saké cup up to my father-in-law, poured it full, and offered it to their company president, who downed it in one gulp and then reciprocated. A sign of mutual respect. They were small cups, but multiplied by 300 . . .

JIZAKE

Jizake is a word often misused to describe a type of saké. In fact, it means nothing more than that a particular saké has been produced by a small brewer in the countryside. A jizake is a "microbrewed" saké, if you will. Lately the word has taken a romantic turn and implies a certain handmade quality and character which may or may not be real. The fact is, any saké not mass produced can qualify to be called a jizake. The term has nothing to do with brewing methods or with quality.

processes. This does not mean it is bad, as there is plenty of fine, reasonably priced Futsu-shu out there.

NAMA SAKÉ

Nama saké (or Namazake; the word *nama* means "fresh" or "raw") is saké that has not been pasteurized (a process called *hi-ire*). Usually, saké is pasteurized twice, once just after brewing and once before bottling (although there are exceptions to this method). When pasteurization is not done, the saké must be kept refrigerated. Any saké of the four major types can be pasteurized or not. Nama saké that is not kept cold can suffer a condition known as *hi-ochi* in which the saké becomes milky and the sweetness and sourness fall way out of balance due to the presence of lactic-acid-producing bacteria.

生酒

What is called **Namachozo** saké is saké that has gone through the pasteurization process only once. Namachozo is stored for the typical six-month aging period as unpasteurized saké and then undergoes pasteurization before shipping. It thus retains some, but not all, of the uniqueness of Nama saké, and is free of the danger of succumbing to the dreaded *hi-ochi*. Another variety, **Namazume** saké, is also pasteurized once, but after brewing and before the aging period.

Nama saké tends to have a fresher and livelier taste complexion than pasteurized saké, but the difference is not always so noticeable.

GENSHU

Genshu is saké that has not been diluted from the naturally-occurring 20% alcohol content it reaches during normal brewing. Most saké is diluted with pure water down to 15–16% alcohol before shipping. If it remains undiluted, the extra 2–3% alcohol can obscure subtler flavors. Some saké can be brewed to a final and naturally occurring alcohol content of less than 20% by adjusting temperatures, using special yeast, or filtering the saké before fermentation is complete. But these lower-alcohol Genshu are not common. **Nama Genshu** is unpasteurized Genshu.

KOSHU

Koshu is aged saké. Saké is usually intended to be consumed within a year of brewing, but there is a slowly growing interest within the industry in aging saké. Although more expensive due to the extra handling it requires, saké aged three, five, and ten years is widely available on the market. Aged saké has a stronger, more astringent, and earthy flavor and aroma to it. At worst, it can be musty and dank. At best, it can be settled, smoky, and rich.

NIGORI SAKÉ

Nigori—"cloudy"—saké (or Nigorizake) is saké that has been roughly filtered so that some of the rice and koji rice in the fermenting tank make it into the bottle. Some breweries will add in the lees to an otherwise filtered product. You must shake the bottle gently to blend the rice lees that have settled to the bottom with the rest of the saké. Nigori sakés are milky in color and almost chewy to taste. They are usually extremely sweet and can be served as "dessert sakés." Before saké filtration technology improved, all sakés were Nigori.

INFUSED SAKÉS

Homebrewers of saké have long been making sakés with a wide variety of flavors. While not commercially available in Japan, these fla-

A friend writes: Once in Japan I was stricken with one of my frequent colds. Despite my misery I went to teach English to two farming families in "the country." When they saw my condition they kept saying, "We have cure! We have cure!" The father went to the back of the house and returned with a huge jar filled with liquid and a large black object spiraling inside. "Drink this. Drink this." Upon closer inspection I realized that the object inside was a 3-foot, curled-up poisonous snake. With their assurances that the concoction was safe and would "cure" me, I drank some directly from the jar with the snake staring me in the face. I don't recall if I was "cured," but I'll never forget when the father later confided that "Grandpa is the only one who drinks *mamushi-zake* [snake-saké]. I take these when I have a cold," and he tossed me a packet of cold tablets.

vored sakés, or "infused sakés," have begun to be produced by saké kura in the United States. Flavors available include Asian Pear, Black Raspberry, Yuzu (Japanese citron), and Roasted Hazelnut. Infused sakés are for people who may not enjoy traditional sakés or who are simply open to new and different tastes.

OTHER SAKÉ TYPES

There are many other saké varieties available, and of course brewers are always trying to single out a brand or process as being in some way special. Some other saké types you may see are:

- **Taru saké** (or Taruzake). This is "cask" or "barrel" saké, that is, saké aged in cypress barrels. The wood imparts a spicy flavor like that of the familiar wooden drinking cup, the masu. The taste is not unpleasant, but it may obscure the "true" saké flavor lurking in the background.

- **Yamahai Shikomi**. These words derive from an older method of saké manufacture wherein lactic acid is not added to the yeast

Is Infused Saké "Real" Saké?

GRIF: Absolutely. Infused saké, where natural flavors have been added to saké, like Black Raspberry, Asian Pear or Roasted Hazelnut, is a new type of saké and deserves its own classification, just like Genshu, Junmai, or Honjozo.

JOHN: Infused saké is no more real saké than wine coolers are real wine. If you have to to add flavor to saké (or wine) to make it taste good, you didn't have very good saké to begin with.

GRIF: Of course, the saké flavor and aroma profile may not meet the traditional profiles set by the Japanese saké industry . . .

JOHN: It is not a matter of tradition, but of common sense. Saké is brewed from rice, just as wine is fermented from grapes.

GRIF: But if it brings in more people so they can then be introduced to more traditional types of saké, then the infused sakés deserve not only their own classification but also to be promoted enthusiastically by the entire saké industry world-wide.

JOHN: The use of additives like flavorings do not constitute a new type, but rather an aberration of the craft.

GRIF: Innovate or die!

starter, or moto. This affects the way the yeast propagates and produces at times a tart yet robust saké.

- **Kimoto.** A process related to Yamahai Shikomi, and producing a similar flavor, involves an intensive mixing and aerating technique applied to the starter mash, again without the addition of lactic acid.

- **Sanzo-shu.** Commercial, undistinguished saké with a heap of sugar, flavoring, and brewer's alcohol added in for economy. Rotgut of a sort. There's no need for you to drink this stuff, although not all of it is as bad as you might think.

Enjoying Saké

ORDERING, BEST BRANDS, BARS & SHOPS

One of the original saké breweries in Hawaii.

Saké Ordering Smarts

When you're at a saké bar or restaurant, the first thing you should do is assess whether or not your server is well informed, since an uninformed server is not likely to help you enjoy or learn more about your saké. This doesn't have to be a confrontational exercise. Just determine who knows more, you or the server. Try dropping a few buzzwords, asking perhaps what kind of Ginjo-shu is available, what good sweet saké or dry saké is available, and so on.

Assuming your server is knowledgeable, describe what you would like. The most significant taste factors are:

- dry vs. sweet
- acidity
- fullness or richness
- fragrant vs. not so fragrant

Another good starting point is temperature. Let the server know if you want a warmed saké, a room-temperature saké, or a slightly chilled saké, as the optimum selection will vary greatly with each range.

It is not inappropriate to ask to see the bottling date (make sure either you or the server can find and read it). In principle, anything over a year old should be avoided. If the storage situation is iffy (for example, if the bottle has been unrefrigerated), consider six months from bottling the upper limit. If the saké has been stored in the bright light, ask for something else!

Selecting Saké in a Store

When shopping for saké, don't go just anywhere. Saké should only be purchased from a shop that stores it properly. While refrigeration is not absolutely necessary, the saké should be kept somewhat cool and not be exposed to too much direct light. As saké becomes more and more available in the U.S., customers are becoming more discerning and dealers are becoming more aware of proper methods of storage.

Naturally, the first step in selecting a saké is to know what you want. Do you want a fragrant saké? Dry, sweet, acidic, mellow? There is fine saké in each of these categories. If a flavor profile description is given under the saké, check it out. If not, ask the shopkeeper or consult this or other English-language books that list sakés by name. Some specialty liquor stores will have an interesting, well-chosen selection, while others may just have a perfunctory offering of whatever their distributor happens to put on the shelf. Your best bet is to be informed and to ask around.

Be sure to check the date of bottling; it should be written somewhere on the label. If the saké has been imported from Japan, you may need to ask for help. Information may be written in kanji characters. and sometimes there is no recognizable numerical date, as years are counted differently in Japan, with year 1 being the first year of an imperial reign. The current era name is Heisei, and since the emperor came to the throne in 1988, recent and near-future date codes on some Japanese bottles can be decoded as follows:

The kanji at the top is commonly seen and means "manufacturing date": in this case, June 1998.

平成 Heisei 10 (1998)
　　　Heisei 11 (1999)
　　　Heisei 12 (2000)
"Heisei" Heisei 13 (2001)

Generally speaking the saké should be **no more than twelve months old** and preferably no more than six months old (as measured from the bottling date on the label). But other factors go into how long a saké can sit. For example, if the saké has been kept refrigerated or in a cool, dark room it can be stored much longer.

If the shop does not seem to have anyone knowledgeable about saké, you are better off waiting than sullying your saké experience.

What to Avoid

Avoid old saké! Again, look for saké less than twelve months old (except, of course, the deliberately aged saké known as Koshu). The fresher the saké the better.

Avoid placing salt tequila-style on the corner of a glass or square wooden masu cup. It may look neat—and have some historical precedent—but the practice is hardly appropriate for today's fine saké.

Avoid warming saké any higher than about 105°F (40°C), moderately warm to the touch. Never warm up premium saké, however; you'll ruin it. (Best to avoid those automatic saké heaters in Japanese restaurants; they're always turned up too high because the owners think Americans demand their saké piping hot.)

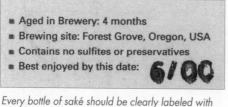

■ Aged in Brewery: 4 months
■ Brewing site: Forest Grove, Oregon, USA
■ Contains no sulfites or preservatives
■ Best enjoyed by this date: **6/00**

Every bottle of saké should be clearly labeled with either a manufacturing or "drink by" date so that you know whether it is fresh.

Avoid saké that is discolored. A light amber tint can be a sign of a fine, rich saké, but a lusterless brown tint can indicate an old saké that has become out of balance and cloying. Although white Nigori saké has been deliberately made to be cloudy, a saké that is not Nigori that has nevertheless become milky white has likely not been handled properly (i.e., it may be an unpasteurized saké that has not been kept cold) and is no longer fit for drinking.

Imports vs. Domestic

Which is better, saké imported from Japan or saké brewed in the U.S.?

In general, if you purchase saké from Japan, look for Honjozo Daiginjo, Honjozo Ginjo, or Tokubetsu Honjozo. These terms refer to high-grade varieties to which a small amount of brewer's alcohol has been added during the brewing process, a standard practice in Japan that has the effect of lightening the saké and enhancing its aroma (☞ see page 34). When it comes to sakés to which no alcohol has been added, Junmai, Junmai Ginjo, and Junmai Daiginjo varieties are what to look for.

Why should you look for quality Honjozo in an import? Two reasons. First, Honjozo saké can be imported but legally cannot be brewed under current Alcohol, Tobacco, and Firearm (ATF) regulations in the U.S. Second, there are many fine saké rices available to brewers in Japan that are just not available to sakémasters in the U.S., so by purchasing a higher-grade imported saké you are almost always purchasing a saké that U.S. brewers simply cannot duplicate.

That said, U.S.-brewed sakés have their own merits. First, they are usually fresher than the imports since the distribution time from the brewery to the consumer is less. Second, U.S.-brewed sakés are less expensive, since the costs of brewing saké, particularly the cost of rice, are 10 to 25% of the same costs in Japan. And since all sakés brewed in the U.S., because of ATF regulations, **must** be brewed using the Junmai method—that is, with no added alcohol—there are some excellent "pure rice" sakés available. (It is rumored, from a reliable source, that late in 2000, we will even see a Junmai Daiginjo produced by a U.S. saké brewery!)

One other factor, of course, is taste. Japanese saké consumers tend to be used to the "koji aroma," while American consumers prefer the "fruity aroma." This is the result of tradition: Japanese have grown up with saké and have more austere tastes, while Americans have grown up with wine, which in general has a much more "fruity" aroma than saké. Sakémasters in the U.S. are adjusting more and more to the desires of the American consumer instead of simply making sakés that appeal to the professional saké judge in Japan.

But remember, always check the "freshness" date on the label to make sure you are buying a "fresh" import or domestic saké. There's nothing worse than an expensive, imported, but "stale" Daiginjo!

THE ECONOMICS OF SAKÉ

Cost analysis explains why several Japanese saké breweries chose to build saké breweries in the U.S. instead of exporting their saké to Americans. In Japan, the most expensive part of making a bottle of saké—as much as 75% of the total—is the rice. Rice is a government-regulated commodity in Japan, which keeps its price, depending on the variety, four to twelve times higher than the world price. In the U.S., rice makes up less than 5% of the cost of a bottle. When you also consider the expense of shipping saké from Japan, it's easy to understand why building a saké brewery in the U.S. makes a lot of sense. Here are the other cost ingredients in order:

IN JAPAN
1. rice
2. labor
3. facilities overhead
4. taxes
5. packaging

IN THE U.S.
1. facilities overhead
2. packaging
3. labor
4. rice
5. taxes

Major saké-producing areas in Japan
and locations of saké breweries in the U.S.

Is Made in Japan Saké "Better" Value Than Made in the USA Saké?

 GRIF: No way! A $65 Daiginjo made in Japan is an absolutely wonderful saké, but so is $9 Junmai Ginjo made in the U.S. But the real question is, "Is the $65 Daiginjo a better value than the U.S. Junmai Ginjo"? Not even close, unless you are one of those very special people who can afford to enjoy $65 Daiginjo every night.

JOHN: You are talking about one saké being a better value than another, then saying not even close unless you can afford it, which is totally irrelevant to the question of which is a "better value." Do not confuse that with quality or goodness. There are many very good sakés brewed in the U.S. Most are quite drinkable indeed, serving the needs of consumers in being refreshing and working well with a wide range of food. However, the U.S. saké-producing world is still in its fledgling stages, as a craft and as a science, and also in terms of raw materials.

GRIF: Many upscale Japanese restaurants in the U.S. refuse to consider even carrying a Made in USA saké because they think the low price will make their customers think they are carrying cheap, low-grade sakés. How ridiculous!

JOHN: Sorry. Same planet, different world. Admittedly, the best U.S.-brewed sakés are better than many Japan-brewed sakés. But the top-grade saké of Japan blows away the best saké in the U.S. by any standards. At least for now.

GRIF: Grrr . . . let the consumers make their choice and watch saké sales soar!

Saké Packages

Maintaining freshness is crucial to the sakémaster as well as to the saké consumer, shopkeeper, and restaurateur. When you're shopping or dining, look at how the saké is packaged or stored, as this makes all the difference in taste.

SCREW TOP VS. CORK

 In Japan and the United States virtually all of the saké available is still sold in bottles with a screw-top closure. The screw top—believe it or not—is actually a superior closure to a cork for saké, but most Americans think it connotes a low-quality, sidewalk wino product. Sakémasters can't use a natural cork because it would discolor the saké. This problem has recently been solved by a bar-top closure made from synthetic cork. It does not discolor the saké, it's easy to open and close, and to Americans it suggests quality on a par with fine wine.

THE BAG IN THE BOX

The traditional bottle for saké in Japan holds 1.8 liters. This is equal to 10 masu, which are 180 ml each (originally the masu was a rice measure). Recently, more and more premium sakés from Japan come in a 720 ml (4 masu) bottle, which is a bit smaller than the standard American-sized 750 ml wine bottle.

The problem with bottles is that once they are opened the saké begins to oxidize. Among ultra-premium sakés, the effect of oxidation can be tasted within only three hours of opening the bottle. The easy solution is to enjoy the complete bottle of saké within two hours, and if you have friends over that's not too hard! But the 1.8-liter bottle, the equivalent of 2½ smaller bottles, presents a bit of a challenge.

Enter the 3-liter "bag in the box." Saké is shipped in a balloon packed inside a rigid cardboard container. As the saké is dispensed from a spigot, the balloon collapses, and since air can't get in, the saké never oxidizes. The bag in the box was first developed in Australia, where 65% of all premium wines are packaged that way. Superior in every way to a bottle, the bag in a box is quite inexpensive compared to the bottle. Unfortunately, too many American wineries decided to adopt the bag in the box and fill it with cheap wine. Americans now perceive that a bag in the box means "cheap."

Why use a bag in the box for saké? It prevents oxidation. It is easy to store in a refrigerator, where you can turn the tap to get a glass of chilled saké. And most important, it allows the saké to be priced at 50% less than the bottled saké to the saké consumer.

Great Saké Bars in North America

A place to drink saké is called an izakaya (but we'll just call it a saké bar). Saké is rarely imbibed without some food as accompaniment (☞ see pages 111–14), so these saké bars are for the most part restaurants with good selections of saké. To qualify as one of our choices for the following listing, a saké bar must carry at least ten premium chilled sakés. Most saké bars, like most saké shops, are Japanese owned and managed, but a few American saké bars are beginning to appear on the scene. Just because a saké bar does not appear on this list doesn't mean there's anything wrong with it. If you have a favorite saké bar that you think should be here, please let us know! (Send updates to sakeexperts@sakes.com.) Be sure to check the freshness of the bottles you are being served from!

PRICE AND SAKÉ

The goal of most saké enthusiasts is to find the best saké at the lowest price. In the U.S. saké industry, sakés are categorized as follows, based on price:

ultra-premium, over $15
super-premium, $10–$14
premium, $7–$9
ordinary, $4–$6
jug, under $4

Excellent sakés can be found in all price ranges, and a good bet is the $7–$10 price range to balance economy and taste. In general, the more expensive sakés are especially suitable for drinking chilled. But in the end it's all a matter of taste.

ARIZONA

Scottsdale

Ra Sushi
3815 N. Scottsdale Rd.
☎ 602-990-9256
Chilled sakés: 10.
Alternative rock and
an energetic young
crowd. Standing bar,
sushi and other Japa-
nese food.

NORTHERN
CALIFORNIA

Carmichael

Saké-Ya
4104 Manzanita Ave.
☎ 916-978-9018
Chilled sakés: 18.
Japanese sushi bar.
Bento box lunch won
raves from the *Sacra-
mento Bee*.

Fair Oaks

Mikuni
4323 Hazel Ave.
☎ 916-961-2616
Chilled sakés: 15.
Five-star Sacramento-
area restaurant with
sushi, unagi, and Japa-
nese salad bar. Be pre-
pared for a wait.

Palo Alto

Jidai-Ya
330 Lytton Ave.

☎ 650-325-2696
Chilled sakés: 10.
Authentic Japanese
decor and crowd.
Fresh sushi and
efficient service.

San Francisco

**Blowfish Sushi To
Die For**
2170 Bryant Ave.
☎ 415-285-3848
Chilled sakés: 25.
Hip artists inhabit this
sleek, dark, loud
Mission District bar
decorated with manga
cels. Sushi and saké
cocktails.

Hana Zen
115 Cyril Magnin St.
☎ 415-421-2101
Chilled sakés: 25.
Stylish restaurant
behind the Nikko
Hotel. Yakitori, sushi,
and vegetable dishes.
Late-night crowd.

Ace Wasabi's
3339 Steiner St.
☎ 415-567-4903
Chilled sakés: 10.
Lively. Boasts its own
web cam, fresh fruit
saké shots, and saké
punch. Loud rock and
roll and "Japanese
tapas."

Sausalito

Sushi Ran
107 Caledonia St.
☎ 415-332-3620
Chilled sakés: 25.
California and Japa-
nese cuisine, intimate
atmosphere, attractive
wood interior. Great
desserts and "over-
flowing masu."

Stanton

Mitsuyoshi
12033 Beach Blvd.
☎ 714-898-2156
Chilled sakés: 15.
Traditional Japanese
food with a good selec-
tion of imported saké.

Sunnyvale

Michikusa
190 S. Frances St.
☎ 408-732-7550
Chilled sakés: 20.
American food.

SOUTHERN
CALIFORNIA

Covina

Bishamon
139 N. Citrus Ave.
☎ 626-967-5900
Chilled sakés: 10.
Friendly atmosphere
with karaoke and a
variety of Japanese

SAKÉ BAR ETIQUETTE

Going into a new saké bar for the first time may be a bit unnerving. It's true, some places do function like private neighborhood bars for expatriate Japanese businessmen, but that's no reason you can't join the club. In the most traditional saké bars you'll know you've arrived when you are asked to sit farthest from the door toward the back of the room, for this is where the high-status guests are seated. But most joints aren't so ceremonious. At a saké bar, it is common (although by no means required) to start with a beer. So the first thing you say to the order taker is "Toriaezu wa beer" or "For now, a beer please." Beer, usually drunk from small glasses so you don't get too full, helps you relax and freshens your palate.

With said beer in hand, you can now peruse the saké menu and food menu in comfort. Some people insist that saké should never be drunk with a meal that includes rice, since saké itself is a rice product. When in doubt, ask your server.

In Japan, it is the custom to never pour for yourself, but since your fine premium saké will be served in its own glass and not a bottle or warmed flask, you will probably not be in a position to pour or be poured for. However, do pour your companion's beer in the beginning. And as the evening wears on, be prepared for lubricated souls to approach your table, flask in hand, offering you a drink. The bar owner may fetch you a small drinking cup to receive this libation. It is permissible to refuse, but often it is more graceful to receive the glass and simply take a very tiny sip in appreciation.

music, including pop and taiko drums. Full Japanese menu with sushi, teriyaki, and tempura.

Fountain Valley

Kappo Honda
18450 Brookhurst St.
☎ 714-964-4629
Chilled sakés: 14.
Traditional Japanese

food. Japanese Pop music. No sushi. Medium lively.

Gardena

Fukuhime
17905 Western Ave.

☎ 310-324-7077
Chilled sakés: 35.
Relaxed clientele with
many Japanese. New
Wave music and an
eclectic menu includ-
ing many sakés and
wines.

Iso Gen
18022 S. Western Ave.
☎ 310-327-5159
Chilled sakés: 10.
Traditional fare with
large officeworker
crowd. Features
imported saké.

Studio City

Asanebo
11941 Ventura Blvd.
☎ 818-760-3348
Chilled sakés: 15.
Cozy neigborhood bar
features Japanese-
Pacific menu, includ-
ing sushi, sashimi, and
many beers and sakés.

Los Angeles

Ita-cho
6775 Santa Monica
Blvd., #3
☎ 323-871-0236
Chilled sakés: 13.
Music: rock and roll
and pop. Lively,
crowded. Japanese
house food: teriyaki
and sashimi.

Torrance

Monjiro
22807 Hawthorne
Blvd.
☎ 310-378-1019
Chilled sakés: 20.
Caters to Japanese
businessmen. Ameri-
can pop and jazz.
Kebabs as well as saké.

Venice

Hama
213 Windward Ave.
☎ 310-396-8783
Chilled sakés: 50.
Big, noisy crowd of
artists, musicians, and
Hollywood types. '70s
music and sushi or
Franco-Japanese food.

COLORADO

Aspen

Taka Sushi
420 E. Hyman Ave.
☎ 970-925-8588
Chilled sakés: 10.
Full service sushi and
Asian cuisine. Reason-
able prices.

Matsuhisa Aspen
303 E. Main St.
☎ 970-544-6628
Chilled sakés: 10.
Expensive, lively
Aspen social scene.
Modern decor with

bamboo and high ceil-
ings. Serves premium
imported and domestic
sakés by the glass.

Kenichi's Aspen
533 E. Hopkins
☎ 970-920-2212
Chilled sakés: 10.
Full-service sushi and
pan-Asian cuisine in
downtown Aspen.
Nightly sushi specials.
Saké sampler: 6 to
taste and compare.

Aurora

Ichiban
3150 S. Peoria St.
☎ 303-755-8900
Chilled sakés: 40.
Teriyaki, udon, tempu-
ra, etc. in a restaurant
setting catering to
officeworkers.

Denver

Sushi Tazu
300 Fillmore St., Unit G
☎ 303-320-1672
Chilled sakés: 15.
Small Cherry Creek
neighborhood place
with excellent sushi.

Tommy Tsumani's
1450 Market St.
303-534-5050
Chilled sakés: 12.
Freshest sushi and
glimpses of glitterati.

A friend writes: One evening, after another thirteen-hour day, I headed to a local izakaya. Alone on this lonely Tuesday, and still not speaking much Japanese, I ordered some food items by pointing at their pictures on the menu, along with a beer. I ate in silence, and began thinking about how the two office workers to my left were enjoying their own happy world, expressing themselves as tipsy Tokyoites are wont to do. I made no attempt at conversation, wallowing in self-pity. Knowing I could never fit in in Japan, never connect. Suddenly, from nowhere, with no warning or additional words, one of the two men ordered an extra glass from the waitress, then pushed it over to me and poured it full of his Junmai-shu. And that was my first taste of simple, pure saké. His gesture turned silent sadness to quiet contemplation, and made all the difference.

Sushi Den
1487 S. Pearl
☎ 303-777-0826
Chilled sakés: 10.
Spacious sushi bar with fresh cuisine and stylish clientele.

Japon
1028 S. Gaylord St.
☎ 303-744-0330
Chilled sakés: 10.
Pleasant decor and reasonable prices. Crowded lunches and dinners. Flexible menu with specialties from experienced sushi chef.

Sonoda's
1620 Market St.

☎ 303-595-9500
Chilled sakés: 10.
Fresh sushi and friendly service. Special holiday menus and happy hour.

Englewood

Samurai
9625 E. Arapahoe Rd.
Suite P
☎ 303-799-9991
Chilled sakés: 20.
Fast, inexpensive, fresh sushi and seafood in a small plaza. Friendly.

Littleton

Sushi Terrace
8162 S. Holly St.

☎ 303-779-7931
Chilled sakés: 10.
Japanese sakés and beers, sashimi, and sushi. Favorites include Tiger Eye, Scorpion Roll, and Dynamite. Handsome dining room and friendly staff.

FLORIDA

Bal Harbour

Yasumoto Bistro
9700 Collins Ave.
Suite 235
☎ 305-861-5475
Chilled sakés: 10.
Sushi bar, world cuisine, and grill in this

North/NW Dade restaurant. Moderately priced. Valet parking.

Miami Beach

Sushi Ko
7971 SW 40th St.
☎ 305-264-6778
Chilled sakés: 20.
Friendly, moderately priced, traditional-style with large Japanese clientele. Open late.

HAWAII

Honolulu

Hakone at Hawaii Prince Hotel
100 Holomoana St.
☎ 808-956-1111
Chilled sakés: 25.
Serene formal dining. Kaiseki and 6-course saké-tasting dinner.

Kyoya
2057 Kalakaua Ave.
☎ 808-947-3911
Chilled sakés: 15.
An elegant, pricey Japanese restaurant on Kalakaua in Waikiki.

Kihei

Hakone at Maui Prince Hotel
5400 Makena Alanui Makena Resort
☎ 808-874-1111

Chilled sakés: 25.
Quiet, graceful surroundings and panoramic views. Tokyo-style sushi bar.

ILLINOIS

Chicago

Sai Café
2010 N. Sheffield
☎ 312-642-9911
Chilled sakés: 10.
The sushi is worth the weekend wait in this Lincoln Park cafe. Small and intimate.

Tsunami
1160 N. Dearborn St.
☎ 312-642-9911
Chilled sakés: 10.
Gold Coast saké lounge attracts a "vogue" crowd. Eclectic Japanese menu includes sushi. Contemporary decor.

Mount Prospect

Torishin
1584 S. Busse Rd.
☎ 847-437-4590
Chilled sakés: 20.
Sushi bar and full Japanese menu. Japanese pop music. Lively crowd and expensive imported sakés.

MASSACHUSETTS

Boston

Tatsukichi
189 State St.
☎ 617-720-2468
Chilled sakés: 20.
Great sushi and excellent bento. Traditional surroundings. Extensive menu, karaoke, and Japanese expatriate crowd.

Ginza
16 Hudson St.
☎ 617-338-2261
Chilled sakés: 10.
Spacious popular restaurant known for great tempura. Traditional service. Sushi, beer, wine, and saké.

Brookline

Ginza
1002 Beacon St.
☎ 617-566-9688
Chilled sakés: 15.
Award-winning sushi bar in Chinatown. Creative maki. Lunch and dinner.

Cambridge

Blue Fin
1815 Massachusetts Ave.
☎ 617-497-8022
Chilled sakés: 10.

Fresh, fast, inexpensive sushi. Japanese beers and sakés.

NEW YORK

New Hyde Park

Kiss'o
1532 Union Turnpike
☎ 516-355-0587
Chilled sakés: 20.
Modern Pacific style in decor and fresh sushi. Weekly saké tasting. Store your own bottle.

New York City

Sakagura
211 E. 43rd St., B1
☎ 212-953-7253
Chilled sakés: 230.
Over 200 sakés in 4 categories. Decor includes "saké shrines."

Decibel
240 E. 9th St.
☎ 212-979-2733
Chilled sakés: 80.
Hip, atmospheric Village "sakéteria." Small, special menu.

Ryoyu
10 E. 52nd St.
☎ 212-759-8484
Chilled sakés: 60.
Moderately priced sushi bar serves lunches and dinners.

Kameda
71 University Place
☎ 212-673-0634
Chilled sakés: 30.
Freshest sashimi and gourmet sushi. Worth the expense.

Denial
46 Grand St.
☎ 212-925-9449
Chilled sakés: 80.
Dark, moody Soho bar displays original paintings. No sushi.

Shabu Tatsu
216 E. 10th St.
☎ 212-477-2972
Chilled sakés: 20.
Worth the wait to cook your own shabu shabu on table grill. Japanese crowd.

Blue Ribbon Sushi
119 Sullivan St.
☎ 212-343-0404
Chilled sakés: 20.
Authentic decor and

fresh sushi and sashimi. Early or late hours sidestep the crowd in this popular Soho establishment.

Chibi's Saké Bar
238 Mott St.
☎ 212-274-0025
Chilled sakés: 15.
Small, intimate candlelit bar attached to the Euro-Japanese Kitchen Club. Appetizers. Serves Koshu and imported brands. Open late.

Inagiku
111 E. 49th St.
☎ 212-355-0440
Chilled sakés: 15.
Elegant, established restaurant in the Waldorf-Astoria. Sushi creations resembling New York landmarks.

Rikyu
210 Columbus Ave.

☎ 212-799-7847
Chilled sakés: 15.
Noisy, friendly family
dining. All-you-can-
eat ("just eat all you
order") sushi for about
$25.

Shabu Shabu
314 E. 70th St.
☎ 212-861-5635
Chilled sakés: 13.
Tabletop barbecue,
sushi, and other dish-
es. Clean and bright.

Bond Street
6 Bond St.
☎ 212-777-2500
Chilled sakés: 12.
Chic, smoke-friendly,
late-night crowd in
Noho. Dozens of sushi
varieties. Lounge, bar,
and 2 tatami rooms.

Nadaman Hakubai
Kitano Hotel
66 Park Ave.
☎ 212-885-7111
Chilled sakés: 12.
A traditional experi-
ence with expensive
kaiseki dinners and
private tatami rooms.

Riki
141 E. 45th St.
☎ 212-986-5604
Chilled sakés: 10.
Sushi bar and full
Japanese menu. Japa-
nese pop and tradi-
tional music. Lively on
weekends; more sub-
dued on weekdays.

Tanokyu
7 W. 46th St.
☎ 212-921-9365
Chilled sakés: 10.
A true izakaya with a

signboard menu and
everyday Japanese
entrees.

OREGON

Hillsboro
Syun
209 NE Lincoln St.
☎ 503-640-3131
Chilled sakés: 40.
Comfortable izakaya
and sushi bar serves
fresh local fish, gyoza,
and tempura with
saké.

PENNSYLVANIA

Philadelphia
Genji
1720 Sanson St.
☎ 215-564-1720
Chilled sakés: 11.
Cool, clean environ-
ment. Very fresh sushi
and a variety of other
dishes.

House of Jin
234–36 W. Chelten Ave.
☎ 215-848-7700
Chilled sakés: 10.
Japanese and Chinese
food. Korean propri-
etors learned food
business in a kosher
restaurant. Sushi and
special entrees. Great
space for parties.

Buddakan
325 Chestnut St.
☎ 215-564-1720
Chilled sakés: 10.
Upscale hot spot. See
and be seen. Fine Pan-
Asian food.

WASHINGTON

Issaquah

Sushiman
670 NW Gilman Blvd.
Suite B-1
☎ 425-391-4295
Chilled sakés: 30.
Clean, new space in
Gilman Corner com-
plex. Near the Yoga
Barn.

Seattle

Mashiko
4725 California SW
☎ 206-935-4339
Chilled sakés: 20.
Spacious. Elegant but
friendly. Lots of sushi
and eclectic music—
bring your favorite
CD.

Nikko
1900 5th Ave.
☎ 206-322-4641
Chilled sakés: 17.
Elegant bar in Westin
Hotel. Very fresh food.
Combo plates.

CANADA

Richmond,
British Columbia

Seto Japanese
Restaurant
125-8291 Alexandra
Rd.
☎ 604-231-9493
Chilled sakés: 10.
Family owned, home-
style cooking, tradi-
tional Japanese style
throughout.

Vancouver,
British Columbia

Shijo Japanese
Restaurant
202-1926 W. 4th Ave.
☎ 604-732-4788
Chilled sakés: 10.
Japanese decor with
sushi bar and tatami
rooms. Modern cui-
sine.

Chiyoda
200-1050 Alberni
☎ 604-688-5050
Chilled sakés: 10.
Traditional cuisine
with sushi bar.

Yoshi on Denman
689 Denman St.
☎ 604-738-8226
Chilled sakés: 15.
Traditional Japanese
with jazz ambience.
Caters to a business

crowd. Features Niiga-
ta jizake.

West Vancouver,
British Columbia

Zen Japanese
Restaurant
2232 Marine Drive
☎ 604-925-0667
Chilled sakés: 10.
Elegant, upscale Japa-
nese-style with sushi
bar, robata, tatami
room. Plays jazz.
Caters to families and
young professionals.

Toronto, Ontario

Katsura
900 York Mills Rd.
☎ 416-444-2511
Chilled sakés: 20.
Large hotel restaurant
(Westin Prince) with
sushi, robatayaki, tep-
panyaki, and other
traditional fare.

Montreal, Quebec

Soto Japanese
Restaurant
3527 St. Laurent St.
☎ 514-842-1150
Chilled sakés: 20.
Japanese eclectic
Fusion cuisine catering
to young professionals.
Intimate atmosphere,
modern music.

Grif's List: Top Brands in the United States

Here is a list of sakés to help get you started on saké tasting. There are more than 350 different sakés sold in the United States, so I've limited my reviews in this section to the sakés that are most widely available (meaning also that these have all been produced in the U.S.; Japan-brewed sakés are usually carried only by large Japanese retailers in major metropolitan areas). If you're a beginning saké taster, these sakés offer a wide range of tastes and styles.

Putting together a recommended saké list has been quite a challenge for me, since I am a firm believer in "to each his own." Plus, as the owner of a saké brewery myself, I naturally favor our own brands. So don't just take my word for it; you should try each saké and decide which one you like best. Information about other, imported sakés available in the U.S. can be found on the Web at www.sakes.com. ☛ See also pages 72–75 for John's tips on sakés from Japan that may be hard to find but are well worth looking for.

For each saké on my list I have provided just enough information (and opinion) to enable you to go out and determine which of these sakés you'd like to try. ☛ See the section on pages 101–2 for ideas on how to host a saké home tasting party where you and your friends can exchange comments.

Remember, the opinions here are my own (and I trust my colleagues in the Saké Association of America won't be too unhappy!).

Let's begin with some general but pointed observations about saké made in the U.S. that have helped guide my rankings. ☛ For an explanation of tasting terms and a discussion of tasting tips, see pages 86–97.

FRESHNESS

Fresh saké is my first priority. Sipping stale saké is a miserable experience, and unfortunately a lot of saké on the shelves in the U.S. is stale. In general, the sakés made in the U.S. are fresher than the sakés imported from Japan. I continue to strongly urge all saké kura in the

U.S. to put freshness dates that are legible and understandable on each and every bottle. (Imported sakés usually show a bottling date, but because this date is sometimes based on the Japanese calendar system that counts "reign years," it is meaningless to non-Japanese consumers.)

VALUE

There are many wonderful sakés made in Japan and imported into the U.S., but they tend to range in price from $20 to $100 per 720 ml bottle. Sakés made in the U.S. range in price from $5 to $20 per 750 ml bottle. In general, you are getting a better value with sakés made in the U.S.

PALATE

Two of the seven saké kura in the U.S., SakéOne and Hakusan, have adapted their sakés to the American palate, which usually prefers a taste and aroma that is closer to wine's than to that of sakés made in Japan. Japanese sakés are made to serve Japanese consumers and may reflect a particular regional style. This doesn't mean that Japanese sakés taste funny or unusual, only that the American-brewed varieties may be a better entry point for beginners.

LABELS

I am passionate about my desire to convey as much information as possible on labels and Web sites and in books or other promotional materials to help educate American consumers about the joys of saké. A good saké label provides useful information about taste, serving suggestions, and ingredients. Not enough labels on either U.S.- or Japan-made sakés work to educate the consumer.

VARIETY

In the U.S., there are twice as many "made in Japan" sakés as there are "made in USA." sakés. With access to a wide variety of saké rices in Japan plus the ability to add brewing alcohol, Japanese sakés, particularly Ginjo and Daiginjo, are much more complex than U.S. sakés.

A friend writes: I can remember my first taste of chilled saké. We were at our favorite hole-in-the-wall sushi shop in Kyushu. The chef's reputation is such that we never order a meal, he just brings what he knows we'll enjoy. I always order warm saké with sushi. Beer fills me up and I miss out on too many tasty morsels. But my brother-in-law insisted that I try chilled saké. I grudgingly did. I was enchanted by it. It tasted slightly sweet yet incredibly light. It went down so easily. It blended perfectly with each bite of sushi. Finally, the chef served us sea urchin on a tiny bed of rice, wrapped in seaweed. That was it. You know the saying . . . "I died and went to heaven!"

I think this gap will close as U.S. saké kura implement more U.S.-grown technology into the art and science of creating great sakés.

BOTTLE SIZE

In the listings here I have favored sakés that are sold in the smaller 750 ml/720 ml and 375 ml/300 ml sizes versus those larger Japan-brewed bottles that hold 1.8 liters. The saké inside those big bottles may be fabulous, but unless you're hosting a mob it's hard to finish it off in one session. I cringe every time I enter a restaurant in the U.S. and see a 1.8 liter saké bottle half filled and sitting on a shelf and not in the refrigerator. DO NOT let the server pour your saké from such a bottle. It is highly probable that the saké is oxidized and stale.

THE LISTINGS

We collected hundreds of media reviews of these sakés, held our own blind saké-tasting competitions (including an adult class in wine appreciation), and then threw in some of my own strong opinions regarding freshness, value, palate, labeling, and bottle size to come up with the following descriptions of sakés in each saké category. The Saké Meter Values (SMV; ☞ see pages 89–90) included with the listings were provided by the breweries and are a rough guide to the dryness/sweetness of the saké. A SMV of ±0 is "neutral," while -6 is sweet and +6 is dry. Remember: use these descriptions only as a guide to help you find your own personal preferences and saké favorites. Enjoy!

JUNMAI DAIGINJO (SERVE CHILLED)

Sad to say, there are currently no American Daiginjo sakés, where the rice is polished to under 50% of the original kernel size. But I expect this to change in the next few years. For now, the only Daiginjo sakés available are imported from Japan. It is pretty hard to go wrong when buying a Daiginjo saké. But please, make sure you know whether it is fresh or not before buying!

JUNMAI GINJO (SERVE CHILLED)

The Junmai Ginjo sakés made in the U.S. tend to be quite smooth in taste with a fragrant aroma. All of the sakés use California rice polished to under 60% of the kernel's original size. Most of the saké tends to be slightly dry with a SMV of 0 to +7.5. These sakés range from $7 to $9 per bottle retail with the exception being the Ozeki priced at around $20.

Momokawa Diamond

SMV: +2. The independent reviewers rate it #1, the blind saké tasting competition ranks it #1, and it is the only saké among the Ginjo sakés with a freshness date, loads of educational information on the labels, and a unique bar top closure (SakéOne brands don't use screw-top closures). A great value at $9.99.

MOMOKAWA DIAMOND

Gekkeikan Haiku

SMV: +3. Very fragrant, smooth, and complex. Gekkeikan, as the #1 saké kura in the world, has produced an outstanding saké from its Folsom, California, kura. But there is no freshness date and little information about the type of saké. Note the cute purple screw top on an elegant frosted green bottle. An excellent value at $9.99.

GEKKEIKAN HAIKU

Ozeki Ginjo Premier

SMV: +7.5. Very smooth with a nice fruity Ginjo-style aroma. It is the driest of the Junmai Ginjo sakés. But at $20 per 720 ml bottle, I think it is about $10 too high. Also, there is no freshness date and absolutely no information in English about the type of saké. The black bottle is elegant, but it makes it absolutely impossible to tell if the saké is stale because you can't see its color.

OZEKI GINJO PREMIER

Shochikubai Ginjo

SMV: +5. Presented in an elegant, cute, white-frosted 300 ml bottle, it is too small for an enthusiastic saké drinker such as myself, but it may be just the right size for saké enthusiasts who are bit more moderate in their saké consumption. It placed well in our blind saké tastings. Unfortunately there is no freshness date and very little information in English on the bottle. A good value at $6.

SHOCHIKUBAI GINJO

Hakushika Ginjo

SMV: +5. The 375 ml clear bottle is in an

unusual plastic wrap that resembles soda pop packaging. A plus of the clear bottle is that you can see the color of the saké and quickly tell if it is stale. I have been told that Hakushika is beginning to print freshness dates on their sakés. Wonderful! There is some information in English. This saké won a gold medal in the International Beer Competition held in Belgium. (Thus prompting the age-old question: Is saké a beer or a wine?) A good value at $6.

HAKUSHIKA GINJO

TOKUBETSU JUNMAI (SERVE CHILLED)

Tokubetsu means "special," which in the case of saké usually indicates that the rice used is polished to less than 70% of its original size. For us heavy saké consumers, knowing that the rice has been polished to less than 65% assures us that the impurities which cause hangovers have been removed and that these sakés, including the Ginjo sakés, will be virtually hangover free. Thinking a bit outside the box, we have decided to include the SakéOne and Hakusan infused or flavored sakés in this category. These infused sakés are new to the world of saké and an example of how American sakémasters are beginning to create sakés that definitely do not fit into the traditional saké mindset in Japan.

Hakusan Napa

SMV: ±0. The Napa brand name refers to Hakusan's saké kura location on the wine tour routes in Napa, California. This saké company has been quite creative with its packaging and

HAKUSAN NAPA

saké brewing due to the fact that its parent company is not a traditional saké brewery. Although this particular sake does not actually identify itself as a Tokubetsu Junmai, based on the information provided by the saké kura we chose to include it in this tasting category. It has the lowest alcohol content of the batch, at 13%, and is very mild. In its elegant frosted green bottle it is a good value at $7 per 750 ml. Unfortunately, there is no freshness date.

Takara Sierra

SMV: +5. Packaged in a striking blue bottle, this is a very smooth and enjoyable saké. Part of the proceeds from sales are donated to the Sierra Club. There is no freshness date. A good value at $3 per 300 ml bottle.

TAKARA SIERRA

Momokawa Silver

SMV: +6. Smooth, assertive, with a hint of herbs. This is the only saké in this category, besides Momokawa Ruby, to use a handcrafted koji rice making process, generally used only in making Daiginjo or Ginjo sakés. A good value at $7.99 for the 750 ml cobalt blue bottle.

MOMOKAWA SILVER

Momokawa Ruby

SMV: ±0. The word we heard to describe this saké over and over was "soft." It is very smooth. An outstanding value at $6.99.

California Ki-Ippon

SMV: +4. Produced in the heart of Los Angeles at the American Pacific Rim saké kura, this saké has the distinction of being brewed by a

MOMOKAWA RUBY

sakémaster who is female. Using Calrose rice polished to 65%, it is the lowest priced saké in this category at $5 for a 750 ml bottle.

CALIFORNIA KIPPON

The Moonstone Line

SMV: -8. All of the Moonstone sakés are 13.5% alcohol and have the same saké base as the Tokubetsu Junmai used in Momokawa's Ruby. They are priced at $7.99 per 750 ml bottle.
Asian Pear: smooth, refreshing, and with an aroma that is very pleasing to the American consumer. **Black Raspberry**: a very "in your face" aroma but fun (one of the tasters, a chef, suggested it be served with lightly prepared pork tenderloin). **Yuzu** (Japanese citron): think "gin and tonic" and serve on the rocks. **Roasted Hazelnut**: only crazy American sakémasters would have thought of this combination. Tasty!

MOMOKAWA MOONSTONE
"HAZELNUT"

Hakusan Plum

SMV: +3. The sweetest of the infused sakés with the lowest alcohol content at 8%. Not as subtle as the Moonstone sakés, but still quite innovative. This is the #1 best selling saké at the Hakusan saké kura. A bargain at $5 for a 750 ml bottle.

JUNMAI NIGORI
(SERVE CHILLED OR ON THE ROCKS)

Nigori sakés made in Japan have a brewing advantage in that distilled alcohol is usually added to them, along with a large amount of sugar to help smooth out the taste and enhance the aroma. Unfortunately, the addition of brewer's alcohol in the U.S. is illegal, so Ameri-

HAKUSAN PLUM

can sakémasters face a major challenge in creating a Nigori that has a pleasing aroma and smooth taste.

Shochikubai Nigori

SMV: -20. Made in the Takara saké kura in Berkeley, Shochikubai Nigori is one of only two Nigori sakés made in the U.S. Priced very reasonably at $5 per 750 ml bottle, it is also available in a 375 ml bottle.

SHOCHIKUBAI NIGORI

Momokawa Pearl (Junmai Nigori Genshu)

SMV: -20. In addition to being roughly filtered it is also uncut with an alcohol content of 18%. Strong hazelnut overtones and very sweet. We enjoy the Nigori Genshu saké as a dessert saké. Wonderful with cheesecake, chocolate torte, and, well, you can experiment! I know from personal experience that it is very challenging to brew this saké so that it has an appealing aroma and a smooth taste. An excellent value at $8.99.

JUNMAI TARU SAKÉ
(SERVE CHILLED OR WARM)

Taru sakés are aged in cedar wood barrels. To our knowledge, Hakushika is the only saké kura in the U.S. making a Taru saké. Not surprisingly, it has a very woody aroma and taste. Since all saké in Japan used to be aged in wood tanks, perhaps the smell of wood brings back genetically ingrained fond memories of one's ancestors enjoying wood-aged saké?

MOMOKAWA PEARL

Hakushika Taru Saké

SMV: +3. This saké suffers the same packaging drawbacks as the Hakushika Ginjo. But as the only one of its kind in the U.S., at $5 per bottle it is definitely worth trying.

HAKUSHIKA TARU SAKÉ

JUNMAI NAMA
(SERVE CHILLED OR ON THE ROCKS)

Nama sakés are either unpasteurized or only pasteurized once. We always thought a Nama saké should only be kept in refrigerated storage and has a shelf life of about four weeks. Yet the Gekkeikan Draft, Shochikubai Nama, and Hakusan Nama, which you see on retail shelves across the U.S., claim to be not pasteurized at all. A big concern, particularly with a Nama saké, is that there are no freshness dates on these bottles. All three of these Nama sakés are priced in the $2–3 range for smaller bottles. Nama sakés in Japan are wonderfully fresh and aromatic, and as long as you can be sure that these U.S.-made Nama sakés are fresh, they can be part of a very enjoyable saké experience.

Gekkeikan Draft

SMV: +4. My saké brewing hat is off to the sakémasters at Gekkeikan for creating a Nama saké that is not pasteurized yet can be sold months after being stocked on room-temperature shelves. Gekkeikan remains the leader among Japanese saké breweries in utilizing new technology. Packaged in a 375 ml bottle, this saké is quite enjoyable.

GEKKEIKAN DRAFT

Hakusan Mild

SMV: +4. Distributed only in the local area of the Hakusan kura in Napa, northern California, this saké comes in an innovative pull-top wide-mouth 250 ml saké bottle. Since it is packaged in a clear bottle it is easy to tell by the color whether or not it is fresh.

HAKUSAN MILD

Shochikubai Nama

SMV: +5. Often seen at sushi stands in super-markets in green 180 ml bottles (we call these sizes One Gulp sakés). Delightful when fresh.

JUNMAI DRY (SERVE WARM)

Americans and Japanese talk dry but drink sweet in both wines and sakés. Yet it appears that many saké drinkers order their sakés based on how dry it is, and the drier the better. Perhaps this preference comes from the beer industry, where the driest Japanese beers have been the biggest sellers. There are many wonderful sakés that are not dry, but then again, each to his own saké preference.

SHOCHIKUBAI NAMA

Hakushika Dry

SMV: +8. The personal favorite of our American saké tasting panel. The packaging has a very Japanese look. Very reasonably priced at $5.50 for the 750 ml bottle.

HAKUSHIKA DRY

Hakusan Premium Dry

SMV: +5. This saké, with a strong koji aroma, was considered quite "Japanese" by the American tasters. The label states that it can be served

HAKUSAN PREMIUM DRY

warm or chilled. Unfortunately there is no freshness date. Reasonably priced at $5.50 per 750 ml bottle.

Ozeki Dry

SMV: +7. Finally! An Ozeki made-in-the-USA saké with a freshness date printed on the front label, albeit in an unobtrusive code. In this case, the freshness date is the bottling date; it is written, for example, as 082798 (August 27, 1998). Reasonably priced at $5.50 per 750 ml bottle.

OZEKI DRY

Shochikubai Dry

SMV: +7. Only available in a 1.5 liter bottle, Shochikubai's Dry saké is best enjoyed when you have a saké party where you can all finish the bottle in one sitting. Reasonably priced at $10.50.

SHOCHIKUBAI DRY

JUNMAI REGULAR (SERVE WARM)

Junmai Regulars account for 90% of the volume of saké produced and sold in the U.S. These are the work horses of the industry and are usually the sakés that are served piping hot in Japanese restaurants out of the 18 liter plastic bag saké warming machines. Priced between $3 and $5 in 750 ml bottles they actually can cost as little as $1 per liter when purchased in the 18 liter package. Calculate out the mark-up of this saké in the restaurant, which then turns around and sells a 360 ml tokkuri for $5, and you can understand why Japanese restaurants push "hot saké"! Several of these sakés are offered in a "Lite" version, which simply means the alcohol content is dropped from 15% to 13%. Extreme price competition means that saké kura are always looking for ways to cut ingredient and brewing costs, and this leaves little room for them to focus on improving taste and quality. There are no freshness dates, and little English information on the labels (in fact, several of the sakés in this category don't even have a back label!). All of these saké kura make quite wonderful Junmai Ginjo and Tokubetsu Junmai sakés, and for an extra $2–$5 per bottle, I would recommend these as being a worthwhile upgrade from the Junmai Regular sakés.

Gekkeikan Original

SMV: +3. The most widely available saké in the U.S., Gekkeikan's standard brew was awarded a 91 rating by the *Wine Enthusiast* in 1994 and won "Best Value" in sakés. Although not to my taste, it obviously has its fans. There is a code printed on the bottle that might be a bottling date, but who knows what KO5B means? A bargain at $4.50 for a 750 ml bottle.

GEKKEIKAN ORIGINAL

Ozeki Regular

SMV: +5. Ozeki and Gekkeikan fiercely compete against each other both in Japan and the U.S. In my opinion the Ozeki Regular is quite similar to Gekkeikan Original. Priced at $4.50 per 750 ml bottle.

OZEKI

Hakushika Regular

SMV: +3. Hakushika has the most automated saké brewery in the U.S., needing only a few skilled workers to run its $40 million kura. This insures a very consistent aroma and taste. Priced at $4.50 per 750 ml bottle.

HAKUSHIKA

Hakusan Regular

SMV: +2. There was a faint code on the front label that might be a bottling date, but I could not figure it out. A bit more elegantly packaged than its competitors with a taste and aroma that is more Americanized. A bargain at $4.50 per 750 ml bottle.

HAKUSAN

Shochikubai Regular

SMV: +3. Cutting costs to the bone, this 750 ml saké doesn't even have a back label, let alone a freshness date. But it is a bargain and you can often get it on sale at $3.50 per bottle. This is the #1 best selling saké in the U.S., based on volume.

SHOCHIKUBAI

A friend writes: Negotiation between the Japanese team and the American team had ground to a halt. It looked like the two sides were so far apart that there was no choice but to cancel the session. Then I looked at the clock and said, "It's saké time!" We brought out the saké, and the Americans began to pour for the Japanese and vice versa and within the hour the atmosphere had changed from outright negative to very positive with many new and creative solutions proposed from both sides. The next morning, we successfully concluded the negotiation—thanks to saké time!

John's List: Sakés Worth the Search

The following eighteen sakés represent a range of the many fine flavor profiles that saké can have. They are all brewed in Japan and, providing they have been cared for properly during shipping and storing, are all wonderful to drink and a great value. Unfortunately, not all of these sakés are so easily found. Although all are available in North America, distribution may not be at the level where all sakés are available everywhere—yet. But things will certainly only improve from here on out. For now, check near you, and also check at any Japanese restaurant you may go to. If you're fortunate enough to find them, the sakés on this list will never let you down. Enjoy the search!

☛ For information on how to read the Japanese labels that may appear on these bottles, see pages 97–101.

Kaiun

Junmai Ginjo, SMV: +5
Light and delicate, with an appealing, flowery nose. A session saké for sure. Doi Brewery, Shizuoka.

KAIUN

Kamoizumi

Junmai Ginjo, SMV: +1
Rich and very full-flavored, with more earthy aspects and robustness than most. Kamoizumi Brewery, Hiroshima.

KAMOIZUMI

Rihaku

Junmai Ginjo, SMV: +3.5
Unique, with an unmistakable touch of fruity richness in the middle of the palate. Rihaku Brewery, Shimane.

RIHAKU

Denshu

Junmai, SMV: +4
Artistic deliberateness is evident in this rich and layered saké. Nishida Brewery, Aomori.

DENSHU

Masuizumi

Junmai Daiginjo, SMV: +5
Well known for balancing a light, flowery flavor and a similarly appealing fragrance. Masuda Brewery, Toyama.

MASUIZUMI

Suigei

Junmai Ginjo, SMV: +8
Dry and very clean, but with a touch of fruitiness in the middle. Fragrantly alive. Suigei Brewery, Kochi.

SUIGEI

Wakatake Onikoroshi

Junmai, SMV: +1
Slightly fruity essence at first fades into a slightly sweet flavor; a crisp tail ties it all off. Omuraya Brewery, Shizuoka.

WAKATAKE ONIKOROSHI

Momokawa

Tokubetsu Honjozo, SMV: +2
Gentle and soft, with a mild lingering sweetness in the recesses. Light, fruity nose. Momokawa Brewery, Aomori.

MOMOKAWA

Masumi

Junmai, SMV: +3
Soft and absorbing, very clean. A session saké with a light fragrance and body. Miyasaka Brewery, Nagano.

MASUMI

Suehiro

"Gensai" Junmai Daiginjo, SMV: +4
Soft and smooth, with most of the goodness in
the recesses of the flavor. Gentle. Suehiro
Brewery, Fukushima.

SUEHIRO "GENSAI"

Nishinoseki

Junmai, SMV: -3
A comparatively sweet saké with a full, rich flavor and nose that fills up all the senses. Kayaji-
ma Brewery, Oita.

NISHINOSEKI

Nanbu Bijin

Junmai, SMV: +1
A great flavor and nose exhibiting the best of a
rice beverage. Sturdy and clean. Kuji Brewery,
Iwate.

NANBU BIJIN

Saké no Hitosuji

Junmai, SMV: +1
An unforgettable berrylike undercurrent and
earthy richness with an enticing nose. Toshi-
mori Brewery, Okayama.

SAKE NO HITOSUJI

Tsukasa Botan

Junmai, SMV: +8
Bone dry and airy, but with a nice substance of
flavor as well. Tsukasa Botan Brewery, Kochi.

TSUKASA BOTAN

Urakasumi

"Zen" Junmai Ginjo, SMV: +2
Dry and a bit soft, with a warming richness of
flavor and a wonderful simplicity. Saura Brewery, Miyagi.

URAKASUMI "ZEN"

THERE'S GOLD IN THEM SAKÉS!

At some point in your quest for the perfect brew you may come across saké with flakes of gold in it. This is Kinpaku-iri saké, and it is sometimes given as a gift. Some say the gold is good for your health, but in fact its main purpose is simply to add a touch of extravagance to the saké, and perhaps several dollars to the cost of the bottle. The gold does not affect the flavor of the saké at all.

Yamatsuru

Junmai Daiginjo, SMV: +8
Clean and elegant, with complexities of flavor and fragrance vying for attention. Nakamoto Brewery, Nara.

YAMATSURU

Shichifukujin

Daiginjo, SMV: +7
Full bodied with a balancing acidity and a nice, rice-based flavor. Kiku no Tsukasa Brewery, Iwate.

SHICHIFUKUJIN

Dewazakura

"Ikko" Junmai, SMV: +3
Crisp and clean with a fat, ricelike richness at the beginning, absorbing into the palate. Dewazakura Brewery, Yamagata.

DEWAZAKURA

Top Saké Shops

The best saké shops in the U.S. tend to be Japanese food and beverage stores, although the number of American stores with a good selection of saké is increasing. We define a "Top Saké Shop" as one that has over twenty types of saké available and is knowledgeable enough to make sure the saké on its shelves is relatively fresh. Still, always double-check the "freshness date." You may find good saké in your local supermarket, which will carry on average four to six different brands. They are usually relatively fresh, since if a saké brand doesn't sell well it will quickly lose its shelf placement.

If you live in one of the thirteen states that allow direct shipments of saké (☞ see page 78), you can order direct from most of the saké breweries in the U.S. or from an Internet saké shop. Send updates or recommendations to add to this list to sakeexperts@sakes.com.

ARIZONA

Tempe
Fujiya Market
1335 W. University Drive
Suite 5
☎ 602-968-1890
Sakés available: 30

NORTHERN CALIFORNIA

Berkeley
Tokyo Fish Market
1220 San Pablo Ave.
☎ 510-524-7243
Sakés available: 40

Concord
Jana Market
1099 Reganti Drive, #A
☎ 925-682-0422
Sakés available: 40

El Cerrito
Yaoya-San
10566 San Pablo Ave.
☎ 510-526-7444
Sakés available: 60

Mountain View
Nijiya Market
143 E. El Camino Real
☎ 650-691-1600
Sakés available: 50

San Francisco
Maruwa Foods

1737 Post St.
☎ 415-563-1901
Sakés available: 150

Uoki K. Sakai
1656 Post St.
☎ 415-921-0514
Sakés available: 50

San Jose
Yaohan
675 Saratoga Ave.
☎ 408-255-6690
Sakés available: 90

Santo Market
☎ 245 E. Taylor St.
408-295-5406
Sakés available: 50

SOUTHERN
CALIFORNIA

Anaheim

Nippon Foods
2935 W. Ball Rd.
☎ 714-826-5321
Sakés available: 40

City of Industry

Nijiya Market
17555 Colima Rd.
☎ 626-913-9991
Sakés available: 30

Costa Mesa

Yaohan
665 Paularino Ave.
☎ 714-557-6699
Sakés available: 35

Fountain Valley

Ebisu Market
18930–40 Brookhurst
St.
☎ 714-962-2108
Sakés available: 60

Gardena

Marukai
1740 W. Artesia Blvd.
☎ 310-660-6300
Sakés available: 80

Pacific Super Market
1620 W. Redondo
Beach Blvd.
☎ 310-323-7696
Sakés available: 50

Los Angeles

Yaohan
333 S. Alameda St.
☎ 213-687-6699
Sakés available: 80

Yaohan
3760 Centinela Ave.
☎ 310-398-2113
Sakés available: 50

San Diego

Yaohan
4240 Kearney Mesa
Rd., #119
☎ 619-569-6699
Sakés available: 40

Nijiya Market
3860 Convoy St., #121
☎ 619-268-3821
Sakés available: 30

San Gabriel

Yaohan
515 W. Las Tunas
Drive
☎ 626-457-2899

Sakés available: 30

Torrance

Yaohan
21515 Western Ave.
☎ 310-782-0335
Sakés available: 100

Nijiya Market
2121 W. 182nd St.
☎ 310-366-7200
Sakés available: 40

Nijiya Market
2533-B Pacific Coast
Hwy.
☎ 310-534-3000
Sakés available: 35

West Los Angeles

Nijiya Market
2130 Sawtelle Blvd.
#105
☎ 310-575-3300
Sakés available: 55

DO YOU LIVE IN ONE OF THESE STATES?

All seven saké breweries in the United States can ship saké direct from the brewery, provided the addressee lives in one of thirteen states where shipping saké via UPS is allowed. These states are:

California	Colorado	Idaho
Illinois	Iowa	Minnesota
Missouri	Nebraska	New Mexico
Oregon	Washington	West Virginia
Wisconsin		

Saké can also be ordered online via the Internet. See the back of this book for listings.

COLORADO

Boulder

Liquor Mart
1750 15th St.
☎ 303-449-3374
Sakés available: 25

Littleton

Lukus Liquor
8457 S. Yosemite
☎ 303-792-2288
Sakés available: 20

Wheatridge

Applejack Liquor
3220 Youngfield
☎ 303-233-3331
Sakés available: 20

HAWAII

Honolulu

Marukai
2310 Kamehameha Hwy.
☎ 808-845-5051
Sakés available: 60

Daiei
801 Kaheka St.
☎ 808-973-4800
Sakés available: 50

ILLINOIS

Arlington Heights

Yaohan Plaza
100 E. Algonquin Rd.
☎ 847-956-6699
Sakés available: 70

Chicago

Sam's
1720 N. Marcey St.
☎ 312-664-4394
Sakés available: 30

MICHIGAN

Novi

One World Market
42705-B Grand River Ave.
☎ 248-374-0844
Sakés available: 40

NEVADA

Las Vegas

Japan Food Express
1155 E. Sahara Ave.
Suite 8

☎ 702-737-0881
Sakés available: 30

NEW JERSEY

Edgewater

Yaohan
595 River Rd.
☎ 201-941-9113
Sakés available: 70

NEW YORK

New York City

Beekman Liquors
500 Lexington Ave.
☎ 212-759-5857
Sakés available: 30

**Park Avenue
Liquor Shop**
292 Madison Ave.
☎ 212-685-2442
Sakés available: 20

**McCabes Wine
and Spirits**
1347 3rd Ave.
☎ 212-737-0790
Sakés available: 20

**Embassy Wines and
Spirits**
796 Lexington Ave.
☎ 212-838-6551
Sakés available: 20

OHIO

Cincinnati

Jungle Jim's

5440 Dixie Hwy.
☎ 513-829-1918
Sakés available: 35

Dublin

Koyama Shoten
5857 Sawmill Rd.
☎ 614-761-8118
Sakés available: 26

OREGON

Beaverton

Uwajimaya
10500 SW Beaverton-
Hillsdale Hwy.
☎ 503-643-4512
Sakés available: 100

Anzen
4021 SW 117th Ave.
Suite E
☎ 503-627-0913
Sakés available: 30

Portland

Anzen
736 NE Martin Luther
King Blvd.
☎ 503-233-5111
Sakés available: 40

TEXAS

Houston

Nippon Daido
11138 Westheimer Rd.
☎ 713-785-0815
Sakés available: 40

Dallas

Danny's Liquor
2001 W. Northwest
Hwy., #120
☎ 972-556-0148
Sakés available: 20

Monticello Liquor
4855 N. Central
☎ 214-520-6618
Sakés available: 40

VIRGINIA

McLean

Naniwa Foods
6730 Curran St.
☎ 703-893-7209
Sakés available: 20

WASHINGTON

Bellevue

Uwajimaya
15555 NE 24th St.
☎ 425-747-9012
Sakés available: 70

Larry's Market
699 120th Ave. NE
☎ 425-453-0600
Sakés available: 20

Kirkland

Larry's Market
12321 120th Place NE

☎ 425-820-2300
Sakés available: 20

North Seattle

Larry's Market
100 Aurora Ave.
☎ 206-527-5333
Sakés available: 20

Seattle

Uwajimaya
519 Sixth Ave. S.
☎ 206-624-6248
Sakés available: 100

CANADA
The following agents can provide information about availability through the government-controlled liquor stores in Canada. Customers can place special orders by phone or

fax for pickup in their local areas.

Barrique Wine Imports
439 Wellington St. W.
Suite 106
Toronto
ONT M5V 1E7
☎ 416-598-0033

Kado Enterprises
1938 Deanhome Rd.
Mississauga
ONT L5J 2K4
☎ 905-822-1340

Featherstone and Company
435-B Berry St.
Winnipeg
MAN R3J 1N6
☎ 204-837-6874

Promark Sourcing
Chesterfield Pl., #F15
North Vancouver
BC V7M 3K3
☎ 604-904-5171

Liquid Art Fine Wines
2233 Burrard St.
Suite 2233
Vancouver
BC V6J 3H9
☎ 604-713-0841

UNITED KINGDOM

Distinctive Drinks
631 Chesterfield Rd.
Sheffield S8 ORX
☎ 0114-255-2002

Saké Breweries in the United States

All told there have been over thirty-six saké kura built in the United States. The first American brewery was established in 1908 as the Honolulu Japanese Saké Brewing Company. At the time Prohibition began in 1920 there were nine saké breweries in the U.S. After Prohibition, another twelve were opened, but all were closed at the beginning of World War Two to conserve rice. (The Hawaii brewery converted to ice cream making and soy sauce.) In 1979 the first of seven modern U.S. saké kura was built in Hollister, California, by the Ozeki Corporation. Since then it is estimated that these seven breweries have invested over $200 million in developing the saké industry in the U.S. These saké breweries are listed below. Most of them welcome visitors, but be sure to call ahead to confirm tasting room and brewery tour schedules.

GEKKEIKAN SAKÉ USA
Main brand: Gekkeikan
1136 Sibley St., Folsom, CA
☎ 916-985-3111
• Tasting room: daily 10–5. Tours: self-guided. Established in 1989, Gekkeikan is the #2 saké brewer in the United States. The parent company, Gekkeikan Brewing in Kyoto, Japan, is the #1 saké brewer in the world with a 5% total market share. The company has developed excellent retail distribution routes in the U.S.

GEKKEIKAN

HAKUSHIKA SAKÉ USA
Main brand: Hakushika
4414 Table Mountain Drive, Golden, CO
☎ 800-303-SAKE (7253)
• Tasting room: daily 10–5. Tours: guided. Established in 1991, Hakushika is the #6 saké

HAKUSHIKA

brewery in the U.S. Its parent company in Japan is the #9 saké brewer in the world. The automated $40 million brewery, in the foothills of the Rocky Mountains, needs only a few employees to operate.

KOHNAN (HAKUSAN)
Main brand: Hakusan
1 Executive Way, Napa, CA
☎ 800-564-6261
• Tasting room: daily 10–5. Tours: self-guided. Established in 1989, Kohnan is the #5 saké brewery in the U.S. and is owned by a large Coca-Cola bottler in Japan. The brewery is strategically located in the heart of the California wine country and boasts an attractive garden.

SAKÉONE
Main brands: Momokawa, Moonstone
820 Elm St., Forest Grove, OR
☎ 800-550-SAKE (7253)
• Tasting room: daily 12–5. Tours: Saturday 12–2.
Established in 1992 to import Momokawa Saké, the saké brewery was built in 1997. SakéOne (formerly the Japan America Beverage Company) is the only American-owned saké brewery in the world. Its focus is on importing and brewing premium saké.

TAKARA SAKÉ USA
Main brand: Shochikubai
708 Addison St., Berkeley, CA
☎ 800-4TAKARA (482-5272)

MICROSAKERY

First came microbreweries in pubs where employees brewed beer to serve fresh from the tanks to their customers. Then came similar miniwineries in restaurants. Now there is a Microsakery, which claims to be able to produce fresh saké for saké bar patrons. Developed jointly by The Brewstore, a Canadian manufacturer specializing in microbreweries and miniwineries, and by SakéOne, a Microsakery may soon be appearing in your neighborhood. Fresh or Nama saké—saké that is not pasteurized—is very difficult for major saké breweries to brew and distribute, since it has a shelf life of less than three weeks and needs to be kept constantly refrigerated. But the Microsakery

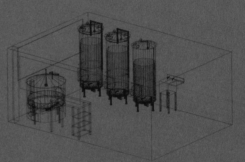

won't have that problem and will be able to turn out excellent fresh saké in small quantities. For contact information, see the back of this book.

• Tasting room and Saké USA Museum: daily 12–6. No tours.

Established in 1982, Takara is the #1 saké brewer in the United States. The parent company in Japan is the #4 saké brewer in the world. Takara's main focus is on selling saké in Japanese restaurants, and it also produces *mirin*, a sweet saké used in cooking. The museum has an attractive display of traditional saké-making tools and equipment.

Sho Chiku Bai
S A K E
松竹梅.

A friend writes: For days northern Vermont had not seen temperatures above −20° Fahrenheit. On these clear days of absolute silence, the sun appears oddly distant, capable of reflecting brilliant light off of the snow, but unable to warm. But sunset would tell another tale entirely, and my adventurous friend and I decided to test our mettle by sleeping under the stars. With numb fingers, we managed to light a small stove, and heat some saké. We crawled into our sleeping bags. Fortified by the saké, we talked through the night, unable to sleep, and trudged home at first light.

The following breweries are not open to the public:

OZEKI SAKÉ USA
Main brand: Ozeki
249 Hillcrest Rd., Hollister, CA
☎ 831-637-9217
Established in 1979, Ozeki is the oldest saké brewery operating in the U.S. and holds the #3 spot in the U.S. market. Its parent company, Ozeki Brewing in Nishinomiya, Japan, is the #3 saké brewer in the world and is well known for its innovative marketing.

OZEKI
SAKE

AMERICAN PACIFIC RIM
Main brand: Ki-Ippon
4732 E. 26th St., Vernon, CA
☎ 323-268-3794
Established in 1987, American Pacific Rim is the #4 saké brewery and importer in the U.S. It is owned by a coalition of Japanese saké breweries in Japan and is well known as an innovative producer of low-cost sakés.

CALIFORNIA
KI-IPPON™
SAKE

Tasting Saké

PROFILES & PREFERENCES

Developing Your Palate

Anyone can enjoy saké at first sip, but to really develop your palate for saké—to learn what you like and don't like—requires tasting experience. Sampling a wide range of sakés is obviously essential here. But if you're intent on becoming a *sake-tsu*—that is, a saké connoisseur—you also need to know how to taste saké and what kinds of things to taste for. Keeping records helps, too; at the end of this book we've provided some blank saké tasting charts that you can use to record your observations.

While you may prefer your premium saké slightly chilled, saké is best appraised at room temperature. This tends to make the various strengths and flaws of a saké most recognizable. You can use a tulip-shaped wine glass for tasting, but since saké is generally not designed to be as bold in its fragrance as wine, a simple tumbler will do just as well. Professional Japanese tasters use a white porcelain cup with a bull's-eye pattern on the bottom to help them better observe the color of the saké.

First, take in the fragrance of the saké and note your observations. Not all saké is meant to have a smell; some is made to have a lively and fruity bouquet. It is all a question of brewing style. Absence of fragrance is not in and of itself a defect.

Hold a sip of saké in your mouth and then suck in a bit of air to release the various flavors and smells. Now, while holding the saké on your tongue, exhale gently. Make sure your breath travels through your nose as well as your mouth. Note the second, almost intuitive fragrance that arises, known as the *fukumi-ka*. This fragrance is an integral part of your saké assessment.

If you are tasting many sakés, you might want to spit the saké out between samples. Swallowing is fine, however, and this affords you a chance to evaluate any aftertaste. Also, you should sip water occasionally to refresh your palate.

But what exactly should you be tasting for?

WHAT IS "BAD" SAKÉ?

Here are some dead giveaways that a saké may be unfit for human consumption:

- unbalanced combination of qualities

- excessive sweetness with no acidity

- something in the flavor that just doesn't belong there

- rubber or paper smell in the fragrance

- bland or flat impact

- dullish gold tinge (unless it is intentionally aged saké)

- old bottling date

- bottle left open or in bright light

The Parameters of Preference

Eight basic parameters—or sensory qualities—can be used to represent the flavor profile of a saké. These parameters are by no means exhaustive or exclusive, but they do help communicate the fundamental elements of a saké, upon which the infinite subtle aspects then dance and interact.

Saké is not wine. Wine and saké have many similarities, but to approach a saké and evaluate it as if it were a wine skews objectivity. You need to be looking for different things. If you get too concerned about the fragrance of a particular saké, you can be disappointed by a saké that was made precisely to not be fragrant. Likewise, some sakés are full and explosive, while others, by design, go out of their way to avoid exactly that.

In the end, it all has to do with what you like. There is nothing more accurate than your own palate and experience in assessing both the profile and quality of a saké. A chart of eight parameters is only a starting point and a quick reference. (Blank tasting charts are included at the back of this book so that you can begin keeping your own saké tasting diary.)

The eight parameters you will be tracking are:

fragrance	none to fragrant
impact	quiet to explosive
sweet/dry	sweet to dry
acidity	soft to puckering
presence	unassuming to full
complexity	straightforward to complex
earthiness	delicate to dank
tail	quickly vanishing to pervasive

These can be arranged in convenient chart form. As you taste a saké, record values for each parameter on the scale along the dotted lines between the words that represent the extremes in each case. Here's what a blank parameter preference chart looks like:

FRAGRANCE	none • • • • • • • • • •	fragrant
IMPACT	quiet • • • • • • • • • •	explosive
SWEET/DRY	sweet • • • • • • • • • •	dry
ACIDITY	soft • • • • • • • • • •	puckering
PRESENCE	unassuming • • • • • • • • • •	full
COMPLEXITY	straightforward • • • • • • • • • •	complex
EARTHINESS	delicate • • • • • • • • • •	dank
TAIL	quickly vanishing • • • • • • • • • •	pervasive

FRAGRANCE

Some sakés have a very prominent fragrance. This is especially true of many premium Daiginjo sakés. Embedded in this aromatic package can be fruit fragrances of all kinds, flowers, ricelike elements, and anything in between. Sometimes the fragrance is gentle and only lasts a few seconds; other times it can be strong and have staying power of a few days.

Some sakés have almost no perceptible smell whatsoever. Quiet, gentle, and straightforward, saké like this survives on its flavor and presence alone.

Neither end of this spectrum is inherently better than the other. The fragrance of a saké is generally a function of the style of a particular region, which in turn is tied to water, rice, and cuisine. Assume, then, that the result was not an accident. Which sakés are better or worse strictly depends on personal preference.

IMPACT

Impact, quiet vs. explosive, is related to the initial impression of a saké immediately after you taste it. Known as *kuchi-atari* in Japanese, it is affected by many things in its production: the pH of the water, the acid content, alcohol content, rice type, milling rate, specific gravity, and so on.

Some saké is soft and gentle, barely making its presence known. Some awaken you out of slumber with an acidity or sweetness exploding across your palate. Some spread flavor into each nook and cranny of your mouth. Some make a narrow and clean beeline for your throat.

Acidity can make a saké spread like wildfire, and alcohol can light up your entire palate—often overly so (which is why most saké is watered down from the naturally occurring 19–20% alcohol to 15–16%).

SWEET/DRY

Although seemingly straightforward, this dimension of a saké can be difficult to put into words. On the most basic level, it is tied in with the Nihonshu-do, also known as the Saké Meter Value (SMV).

The SMV is a measure of the specific gravity of a saké, that is, the ratio of the density of the saké in relation to the density of pure water. Basically, and this is a gross oversimplification, you can say that the more unfermented sugar there is in the saké, the more dense it is. The scale used by brewers for the SMV is open-ended but generally runs

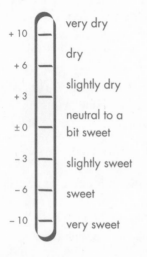

+ 10 — very dry

+ 6 — dry

+ 3 — slightly dry

± 0 — neutral to a bit sweet

– 3 — slightly sweet

– 6 — sweet

– 10 — very sweet

SAKÉ METER VALUE (NIHONSHU--DO)

A representation of the hydrometer used to measure the Saké Meter Value (Nihonshu-do) of a saké is often printed on the label, with the values presented in a vertical scale. Toward the top is dry; toward the bottom is sweet. The SMV, despite its widespread use, is not the best predictor of how a saké will actually taste. Other factors like acidity and temperature are also important.

from –6 to +10 or so, with numbers assigned so that lower or negative numbers indicate increasing sweetness, and higher, positive numbers indicate drier saké. (Our Parameter Preference Chart similarly has sweet on the left and dry on the right so that it is consistent with the logic of the Nihonshu-do scale.) Originally, ±0 was considered neutral, but as taste perceptions and preferences have changed drastically over the last few decades, +2 or so is now considered a neutral value.

The SMV is far from being the only factor affecting the impression of sweet or dry. Acidity plays a huge role, and saké with higher acidity will generally taste drier than the numbers alone would indicate. Similarly, a saké with lower than usual levels of acid can taste a tad sweeter than the SMV would suggest. Other factors contributing to the perception of sweet/dry are temperature, what you've been eating, and what other saké you've been tasting.

ACIDITY

Acidity in saké is measured as the number of milliliters of a base chemical needed to neutralize 10 ml of saké. What, you're not carrying your chemistry kit? Just keep in mind that the number is usually from 0.8 to 1.7. This is not a huge range, and the really important thing to keep in mind is that perception of acidity does not always directly correlate to actual acid content. A sweeter, rougher saké may not taste as acidic as a drier saké with the same acidity.

Acidity can make its presence felt most noticeably at the beginning and at the end; in between it helps spread everything about. Saké with higher acidity often stands up better to oilier foods like tempura or fish (raw or cooked!). Rich-flavored or rather salty side dishes may not need all that acid, and in fact will work better with a lower-acidity saké.

PRESENCE

Presence could also be called body, or even richness. Saké is in general a light beverage, even compared to the lightest of wines. Presence thus refers to the mouth feel, the graininess against your tongue, and the viscosity or lack thereof. It can range from unassuming, quiet, light, airy, and delicate on one end, to full-bodied, fat, heavy, thick, and ripe on the other. Some saké are smooth and airy; some are rich and creamy. Note that Nama saké (unpasteurized saké) generally has a much more prominent presence than saké that has been pasteurized.

COMPLEXITY

Some sakés are very straightforward. Boom. Full stop. This can be very reassuring and sometimes exactly what you want. If the conversation is likely to be lively and loud, no one's going to feel like pondering the layered contours of the saké you are tasting. Simple but solid saké is what you need.

Other sakés are intricate and complexly structured, or *okubukai* in Japanese. The quieter you get and the more attention you pay, the more flavors and sensations present themselves to your mouth, nose, and mind. Layer upon layer of subtly interconnected sensations unfold from the depths of the flavor profile. Some say this kind of saké represents the pinnacle of saké brewing and tasting.

Both the straightforward, simple, and easy-to-drink saké and the wildly complex saké have their place. Do not confuse complexity with purity, however. Purity can be defined as the absence of inappropriate and out-of-place off-flavors. A saké can thus be immensely complex but still have no flavor element that doesn't belong there; complex but pure.

EARTHINESS

Some saké has elements that are bitter, dank, tart, dark, or heavy. The best Japanese term is *koku ga aru*, although a direct translation will not make it through unscathed. The opposite of "dank" saké is not so much light and delicate saké as it is saké that doesn't display these darker attributes so readily.

Aged saké often has earthiness as part of its flavor profile. So does, not without exception, saké from the southern part of Japan. Words like "earthy" and "dank" may connote an image of a good, hefty twenty-year-old distilled beverage, but remember that saké is essentially a light beverage. So earthiness in saké is subtle, very subtle, but it's enough to be noticed and worthy of comment.

TAIL

Does the saké flavor jump ship and disappear from your mouth and throat in an instant, leaving you feeling somewhat rejected? Or, does it linger and hang out, the puckering acidity or stubborn sweetness remaining to be savored for minutes afterward? A saké tail (*kire* in Japanese) can run the gamut from clean, crisp, sharp, and vanishing to lingering, puckering, and friend-for-life pervasive. If a saké's flavor is pleasing, it only makes sense that you should want it around a little longer.

Typical Flavor Profiles

You can use the parameter preference chart described above to "score" individual sakés. In this section, we've used it to try to isolate and express what we believe are the basic differences among the major

A friend writes: I was dating a Japanese man whose family runs a saké brewery. One night, he took me to a traditional Japanese izakaya with an extraordinary selection of saké. "Would you like to learn about saké tonight?" he asked. I accepted, and without hesitation he ordered. We sat there for hours toasting ourselves into a wonderful fog. Later, in the middle of a conversation about politics, suddenly, I burst out with, "I want to make love to you tonight!" He stared at the bar, carefully took his cup of saké, and calmly sipped it, then smiled and said, "I'll get the bill." P.S.—Now we're married.

types of saké. What classification a saké fits into depends on how much of the rice grain is used and whether or not brewer's alcohol is added to the final brew. Thus, very broadly speaking, there are four types of saké (☛ see also pages 22–33 for information about the brewing process):

- Junmai: rice only
- Honjozo: a tad of distilled alcohol added
- Ginjo: highly milled rice, with or without alcohol added
- Daiginjo: even more highly milled rice, with or without added alcohol

Each saké type's general flavor profile derives from the brewing methods employed. But there is a lot of overlap between the types, and very often you simply cannot tell what you're drinking. Some sakés taste above their class (or are just different), and others don't live up to the billing (or are just different). And there are many other factors that come into play as well: rice, water, the skill of the brewers. It is practically impossible to determine how a saké will taste based on which "type" it is, or to fault it when it doesn't fit the mold.

That said, generalities can be useful as you try to nurture your understanding of saké and develop your palate.

JUNMAI

Junmai saké often has a fuller, richer body and an acidity that is higher than average. The fragrance (what wine tasters call the nose) is often not as prominent as in other types of saké, and still other parameters are not dependent on whether a saké is a Junmai or not. A representative Junmai flavor profile is strong impact, neither sweet nor dry, lots of presence, but relatively straightforward. Thus:

Parameter	Low	Scale	High
FRAGRANCE	none	· · ■ · · · · · · ·	fragrant
IMPACT	quiet	· · · · · · ■ · · ·	explosive
SWEET/DRY	sweet	· · · · ■ · · · · ·	dry
ACIDITY	soft	· · · · · · · · ■ ·	puckering
PRESENCE	unassuming	· · · · · · · · ■ ·	full
COMPLEXITY	straightforward	· · ■ · · · · · · ·	complex
EARTHINESS	delicate	· · · · ■ · · · · ·	dank
TAIL	quickly vanishing	· · · · · ■ · · · ·	pervasive

HONJOZO

Honjozo saké is often a bit lighter, due to the small amount of grain alcohol added at the end of the ferment. Remember that this is not a bad thing, in moderation, and brewers have been doing it for hundreds of years. It is **not** simply a cost-cutting measure when used properly and to achieve the intended effect. The flavor is lighter, and magically the fragrance becomes much more prominent. Here is a representative Honjozo saké:

Parameter	Low	Scale	High
FRAGRANCE	none	· · · · · · ■ · · ·	fragrant
IMPACT	quiet	· · · ■ · · · · · ·	explosive
SWEET/DRY	sweet	· · · ■ · · · · · ·	dry
ACIDITY	soft	· · ■ · · · · · · ·	puckering
PRESENCE	unassuming	· · ■ · · · · · · ·	full
COMPLEXITY	straightforward	· · · · · · ■ · · ·	complex
EARTHINESS	delicate	· · · · · · · ■ · ·	dank
TAIL	quickly vanishing	· · · · · · · ■ · ·	pervasive

GINJO

Ginjo saké is much more delicate, light, and complex than the above two. Why? The rice has had the outer 40% of the grain polished away, leaving the inner 60%, as opposed to leaving 70% for Junnmai and Honjozo. Special yeast, lower fermentation temperatures, and labor-intensive techniques also make for fragrant, intricate brews. Here is a typical Ginjo chart, clearly showing the mix of delicacy, complexity, and fragrance.

FRAGRANCE	none	•	•	•	•	•	•	•	•	■	•	fragrant
IMPACT	quiet	•	•	•	•	■	•	•	•	•	•	explosive
SWEET/DRY	sweet	•	•	•	•	■	•	•	•	•	•	dry
ACIDITY	soft	•	•	•	■	•	•	•	•	•	•	puckering
PRESENCE	unassuming	•	•	•	■	•	•	•	•	•	•	full
COMPLEXITY	straightforward	•	•	•	•	•	•	•	•	■	•	complex
EARTHINESS	delicate	•	■	•	•	•	•	•	•	•	•	dank
TAIL	quickly vanishing	•	•	•	■	•	•	•	•	•	•	pervasive

DAIGINJO

Finally, there is Daiginjo. This is basically an extension of Ginjo. The rice has been milled so that no more than 50% of the original size of the grain remains, although this often goes to 35%, and even more care is taken to create saké representative of the pinnacle of the craft. Although there is a range of Daiginjo styles, here is a somewhat typical example, powerfully fragrant and complex:

FRAGRANCE	none	•	•	•	•	•	•	•	•	•	■	fragrant
IMPACT	quiet	•	•	•	•	■	•	•	•	•	•	explosive
SWEET/DRY	sweet	•	•	•	•	■	•	•	•	•	•	dry
ACIDITY	soft	•	•	•	■	•	•	•	•	•	•	puckering
PRESENCE	unassuming	•	•	•	•	•	•	•	■	•	•	full
COMPLEXITY	straightforward	•	•	•	•	•	•	•	•	•	■	complex
EARTHINESS	delicate	•	•	•	•	■	•	•	•	•	•	dank
TAIL	quickly vanishing	•	■	•	•	•	•	•	•	•	•	pervasive

Tasting Words

Tasting saké is like tasting wine, cigars, coffee, chocolate, or anything else that calls for a bit more attention than usual in order to catch the complexity of flavors and sensations. By definition it is an extremely subjective exercise. Not only what people taste and smell but also how those sensations are expressed will vary from person to person, place to place, and minute to minute.

There is no end to the number of possible terms that can be used for the saké-tasting experience. But we need to start somewhere, so here are the basic groups of Japanese terms that are commonly used, along with their English equivalents. The Japanese terms are useful because they indicate which taste aspects are considered especially important when assessing saké.

GOOD

amai, amakuchi	sweet
karai, karakuchi	dry
nameraka	smooth/soft
nigai	bitter
shibui	somewhere between acidic and astringent
suppai	sour
sanmi	acidity, presence of acid in the flavor
umami	a very difficult term to translate directly, as it's not a taste sensation; basically it's what makes you say, "Mm, that's good. Let's have some more of that!"
kirei	clean, nothing extraneous
koku ga aru	an earthy aspect to the flavor, perhaps bitter or slightly tart heaviness
maruyaka	well rounded, a full-flavor package
okubukai	intricate, complex

fukurami	a flavor that spreads across your palate
fukumi-ka	the subtle fragrance that appears in your senses when you take a sip of saké and hold it on your tongue and exhale

NEUTRAL

hosoi	a narrow bandwidth of flavor
karui	light
omoi	heavy

BAD

gomu-shu	smell of rubber
hine-shu	old smell, musty touch
kabi-shu	mold smell
kami-shu	paper smell
arai	rough
kitsui	harsh
kudoi	cloying
usui	thin
zatsumi ga oi	lots of off-flavors, flavors that do not belong

Reading Japanese Saké Labels

Reading Japanese saké labels can be tricky for many reasons. Naturally, the linguistic barrier rises high in the form of the Japanese writing system. Thousands of characters are in everyday use in Japan, but some characters are unique to the saké world and cannot be read by most Japanese at first glance either. Add to this the tendency to use artistic as opposed to cleanly legible calligraphy, and reliable label reading becomes even more difficult.

The somewhat good news here is that what is usually written on a

At right is a fairly detailed label for a Japanese regional saké. The characters you see in the left column are those used on most other Japanese imports and can thus be used as "decoders" when trying to figure out label content. American-produced saké labels are printed entirely in English but may not contain quite as much detail about the saké and its particular attributes.

1. gold medal winner
2. variety: Daiginjo
3. brand name (*meigara*): Kome no Sasayaki
4. ingredient code: YK-35A-35B [explained below]

The middle of the label contains the key details to look for. Most saké labels contain this sort of information, but often in a different order. Some labels suggest optimum drinking temperatures.

5. rice: Yamadanishiki (Premium Grade): 100%
6. rice production: Hyogo Prefecture, Special A Zone
7. *seimai-buai*, or polishing percentage (how much the rice was polished before brewing); in this instance, rice for the shubo (starter) and koji was polished to 35%, as was the rice for brewing
8. yeast: Kumamoto Saké Brewing Research Laboratory Yeast #9
9. brewing period: 35 days
10. alcohol: 17.5%
11. Saké Meter Value (Nihonshu-do): = +4.0 (slightly dry)
12. acidity: 1.3
13. amino acidity: 0.9
14. brewer's name: Mutsuro Sasaki
15. brewer's "style": Iwate Prefecture, Nanbu school
16. storage temperature: −3°C [27°F]

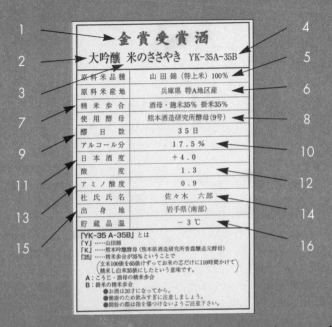

金賞受賞酒

大吟醸 米のささやき　YK-35A-35B

原料米品種	山田錦（特上米）100%
原料米産地	兵庫県 特A地区産
精米歩合	酒母・麹米35% 掛米35%
使用酵母	熊本酒造研究所酵母(9号)
醪 日 数	3 5 日
アルコール分	1 7 . 5 ％
日本酒度	＋４．０
酸　度	1 . 3
アミノ酸度	0 . 9
杜氏氏名	佐々木　六郎
出 身 地	岩手県(南部)
貯蔵品温	－ 3 ℃

「YK-35 A-35B」とは
「Y」……山田錦
「K」……熊本吟醸酵母（熊本県酒造研究所香露醸造元酵母）
「35」……精米歩合が35％ということで
（玄米100俵を65俵けずってお米の芯だけに110時間かけて精米し白米35俵にしたという意味です。）
A：こうじ・酒母の精米歩合
B：掛米の精米歩合
●お酒は20才になってから。
●健康のため飲みすぎに注意しましょう。
●開栓の際は指を傷つけないようご注意下さい。

The bottom of the label is taken up by a lengthy explanation of the ingredients code at the top: Y = type of rice; K = yeast type; 35 = polishing % (A = % for koji and shubo rice; B = % for other rice).

There are three cautionary notes at the very bottom of the label:

- Saké is for those 20 years old and up
- For your good health, drink in moderation
- Be careful not to injure your hand when opening the bottle

The front of a saké label may be attractive, but it often doesn't provide any information about ingredients or taste. The label at left indicates only the following:

- *brand name: Kudoki Jozu*
- *type: Junmai Ginjo*
- *brewery: Kamenoi Saké Brewery, Inc.*

Should the U.S. Accept the Japanese Saké Classification System?

GRIF: No way. In Japan, the Ginjo and Daiginjo classifications are based primarily on what percent of the saké rice has been milled off. But in the U.S. there is little quality saké rice available, so no matter how much you mill the rice, it is still a table rice and not a saké rice.

JOHN: There is no need for the U.S. to reinvent the wheel. The Japanese classification is based on factors that make a difference in the final flavor. It makes it easier for consumers to know what they are buying. Is this not the point?

GRIF: The saké industry in the U.S. should adopt a saké classification system that makes sense to Americans in the U.S. For example, why not just allow the Ginjo classification for sakés that are using certified saké rice?

JOHN: But then you're back to rice types. The Junmai-Honjozo-Ginjo system is not sacred or traditionally honored, it just makes sense. Plain and simple.

label, and what must be written on a label, is limited to a handful of easily recognizable terms. So if you have the time and patience, you can learn to recognize the patterns and figure out what kind of saké you have, even if you can't read the name of the saké itself.

However, this is complicated by the fact that, although there are regulations regarding content, there are none regarding the placement or size of the characters conveying that content. Some kura will print the name of the saké in huge characters and the grade (Junmai Ginjo, for example) in small, seemingly insignificant characters along the side. Another saké will have the fact that it is a Daiginjo saké splashed larger than life across the label, with the brand name tucked into a corner, almost as an afterthought. It is all a matter of style.

Fortunately, in the U.S., we are saved by the back label. By law, the name of the saké must be printed on the back label in English, along with other pertinent information like alcohol content and ingredients. Many brewers are taking advantage of this space to educate Americans by including information about the rice, milling rate, and Nihonshu-do (SMV; ☞ see pages 89–90). Although it is not legally required to put classifications like Honjozo, Junmai, and Ginjo there, most kura want to convey that information and willingly provide it.

So enjoy the beauty of the native Japanese label, but get your information from around the back.

Saké Home Party Plan

Having friends over to taste a variety of sakés is a great way to expand your knowledge of saké and discover what you like. Here are some suggestions for how to organize a successful home saké-tasting party.

TYPES OF SAKÉ

Pick a minimum of four sakés to taste, although more is always better. Make sure the sakés are fresh! For the best taste contrasts, select a dry saké (*karakuchi*), a slightly sweet saké (*amakuchi*), a full bodied complex saké (Junmai Ginjo), and an unfiltered saké (Nigori).

TYPES OF FOOD

Provide a variety of simple foods that range from bland to spicy, sour to sweet, robust to delicate. Fruits, vegetables, cheeses, lightly prepared fish, chicken, and pork all offer different taste sensations when combined with saké. And you will be amazed how different a single saké can taste, depending on what you have just eaten. The more food served with the saké, the longer your saké tasting party will stay manageable!

GLASSWARE

Sample using 2 ounces poured into a regular wine glass. If possible, use a different wine glass for each saké for each person. As an alternative, have a water pitcher available to rinse out the glasses between sakés. Also provide a pitcher to collect any saké remaining in the glass

SAKÉMASTER PROGRAMS

Did you know that there are now more certified wine sommeliers in Japan than there are in France? We expect the same trend to be repeated with saké, with more certified sakémasters in the United States than in Japan. Currently there are two saké sommelier or sakémaster programs being developed in the United States. One is sponsored by the Saké Service Institute (SSI), which has certified more than 10,000 Japanese as saké sommeliers in Japan. The second certification program is sponsored by the International Saké Institute's Saké Resource Center (SRC), which is based in the U.S. SRC's sakémaster program has not officially started up yet, but it will have four levels of certification, with the highest level actually requiring candidates to obtain hands-on experience by working for a short period of time as a sakémaster in a saké kura in the U.S.

before a new saké is poured in. Guests shouldn't feel they have to drink all the saké set before them.

TASTING

Follow the instructions ☞ on page 86 to fully "taste" the saké, as opposed to just drinking it. You can swallow the saké to check the aftertaste, or spit it out (elegantly) into the pitcher. Sip some water to rinse out your mouth before moving on to the next tasting.

EDUCATION

Begin the tasting party by asking your guests what they know about saké. Then share some of the knowledge you have gained from this book. Once people begin tasting, ask them what the saké's flavor and aroma remind them of. You will be amazed at how many different flavor components your guests will identify.

Timing: About ten minutes of talk and twenty minutes of organized tasting are just right. After that, relax and enjoy the food and saké without worrying too much about formalities.

SERVING SAKÉ

ETIQUETTE, COCKTAILS, FOOD

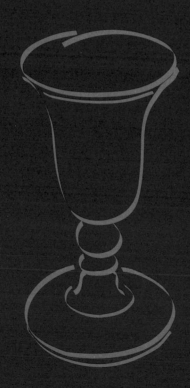

How Should You Serve Saké?

Saké has traditionally been served warm. Advances in brewing technology have led to saké flavor profiles that are destroyed by heat, so that nowadays most premium saké tastes best when it is slightly chilled. If saké is too chilled, however, many of its flavor components are masked, just as a wine's would be. Saké, also like wine, presents a different personality at different temperatures. Each saké has its own optimum temperature, and this will vary, with the saké as well as your personal preference. As a general guideline and starting point, consider the following:

- Ginjo and other premium sakés are good lightly chilled.

- Junmai, with its slightly fuller flavor and slightly higher acidity, often comes into its own slightly cool or at room temperature.

- Saké that is warmed should not be too hot, but rather just above body temperature, about 100–104°F (38–40°C).

- For some, piping hot saké simply holds its own charm, and flavor be damned. If that's your poison, try it at 104–30°F (40–54°C).

Saké is easily warmed by placing a filled flask in a saucepan of hot water or in a microwave. However, allowing a chilled saké to warm up and into room temperature, tasting it all the while, is an excellent way to find what works best for a given saké. It will help you match it with food as well as determine your own preferences.

Pouring Etiquette

With saké as with beer, pouring for others is a common custom in Japan that takes a bit of getting used to but has a wonderful charm and appeal once ingrained. Small cups (called ochoko) and a larger serving flask or vessel (tokkuri) allow for frequent refill opportunities, each of which is a miniritual of social bonding. In formal situations,

A friend writes: While in Japan my fiancée and I fretted about how to announce our engagement to my visiting parents. One day, the ladies of my English class had a party for them. My students seemed to speak better English with each sip of saké. After a while, the boldest of my students pulled my mother close to her and said, "You are proud of Michael to marry Kelly. No?" In the following silence, my Mother slowly turned to face us. Kelly and I were grinning madly. My mother then reached over to give Kelly a hug. "Of course we are, my dear," she smiled, "of course we are." We ordered more saké, and the party became a celebration.

the tokkuri is held with two hands when pouring. Likewise, the person receiving should lift his or her glass off the table, holding it with one hand and supporting it with the other.

The more formal the situation the more such etiquette is observed. Even in informal situations, pouring saké for one's table companions is the norm, although pouring and receiving parties generally revert to the more natural one-hand grip. Among close friends, after the first round or so, all pouring rituals are often abandoned for the sake of convenience. Pouring for yourself is known as *tejaku*.

Your companions may feel an uncontrollable urge to refill your cup when it is empty. Resisting their entreaties for more is generally futile, so the best approach is to allow your cup to be filled and then take tiny, tiny sips so that it never goes dry.

And while this is a book about saké, we recognize that there may be times when you just aren't up for imbibing. Pleading illness or pharmaceutical conflict is an acceptable excuse, and if you're among strangers it is quite permissible to simply say something like "Alcohol and I simply don't agree" or "I'm allergic to saké." White lies of this sort, when in Japan at least, are far preferable to saying that you just don't feel like drinking—even when everyone **knows** it's a white lie.

Sakéware

There are as many saké-drinking implements as there are brands of saké. Some more common terms and types are:

- Tokkuri: The typical ceramic flask used to warm and serve saké, with a narrow neck for retaining heat. Tokkuri come in all shapes and sizes: round, long and narrow, and anywhere in between.

- Ochoko: Small saké cups of myriad color and design, often of traditional Japanese pottery like Bizen or Shigaraki ware. The cups broaden at the top to allow the delicate fragrance of the saké to waft gently up.

- Guinomi: Small cups—often fluted at the edge—a bit bigger than ochoko. These come in all styles and can be great works of art.

- Masu: A square cedar box holding 180 ml, originally designed as a rice measure. A thousand masu equal one *koku*, which in Japan's feudal age was considered to be the amount of rice needed to feed one person for one year. The *koku* thus became the standard for valuing the stipends allotted to the samurai. Years ago, the masu was indeed the most commonly used "cup" for drinking saké. But no one really drinks regularly from masu anymore, as the

smell and flavor of the wood over-
power today's delicate sakés. If, for
the sake of tradition, a masu is
required, a glass liner is often insert-
ed beforehand to prevent the saké
from absorbing the flavors of the
bare wood. (It must be said that the
cedar does impart a cinnamonlike

flavor that on its own is not unpleasant, although it may obscure
the delicate flavor of the saké.)

- Wine glasses and simple tumblers: While not traditional, tulip-
  shaped wine glasses do a wonderful job of concentrating the

aromas of saké. They also allow for
scrutinizing appreciation of the
saké's golden tint, or lack thereof.
Because the fragrance of saké is not
as prevalent as that of wine, a stan-
dard tumbler with straight sides will usually do just fine.

- The martini glass, the beer mug, the champagne glass, the
  Chardonnay glass, the Bordeaux glass . . . every major type of
  alcoholic beverage has its own recognizable glass from which to
  enjoy it. Right now, the saké industry is wishy-washy with some
  people saying a masu is good and others saying a wine glass is
  better; yet others are stuck on traditional
  ceramic ochoko. It is rumored that a new
  saké glass is being developed by saké
  enthusiasts in conjunction with leading
  European glassware manufacturers. Just
  as a certain shape of glass is easily identified as a champagne glass or a martini
  glass, we may soon be introduced to a
  specialty saké glass.

STORE NOW, DRINK LATER

Saké is fairly delicate. The rules for storing saké and keeping it drinkable are simple and easy to remember, if not always so easy to implement.

Light is bad for saké, pure and simple. That's why almost all saké bottles are brown, blue, or green. Even so, keeping these UV-protected bottles out of strong light is just good practice. Direct sunlight especially will adversely affect saké in all but the most opaque of bottles.

The next villain is temperature. Although there is no single ideal storage temperature, keeping most sakés below 50°F (10°C or so) is a good rule of thumb. The best solution is to keep your saké in the refrigerator.

Most saké will, however, survive storage at room temperature, provided the temperature is kept steady and the saké is not kept there too long (a couple of weeks at most). The finer and more delicate a saké, the more it can benefit from being stored at colder temperatures, even as low as 43°F (6°C).

If a saké is not pasteurized (that is, if it is Nama saké), it stands a very good chance of going bad if not kept refrigerated. It can become cloudy and cloying and way out of balance. This condition is known as *hi-ochi*; only unpasteurized saké is susceptible to this kind of deterioration.

WHAT'S IN A SAKÉ NAME?

Saké names almost always have a story behind them. Many are taken from a nearby mountain or lake. Often, Chinese characters considered auspicious are used in combinations. Most common are characters for "mountain" (pronounced *san* or *yama*, depending on how it is used), "crane" (*tsuru*), and "chrysanthemum" (*kiku*).

One particularly interesting saké name is Mado no Ume, or "Plum of the Window," from Saga Prefecture. The story has it that over a hundred years ago a plum branch snaked its way in through the window of the brewery, and a blossom fell into a fermenting tank. The resulting saké was outstanding, prompting the owner to adopt the name for posterity.

Other saké names you might see, with their literal translations, are:

Shochikubai	Pine, Bamboo, Plum
Onigoroshi	Demon Slayer
Shikizakura	Four-Season Cherry
Kikuhime	Chrysanthemum Princess
Hakusan	White Mountain
Gekkeikan	Laurel-Wreath Crown
Hakushika	White Deer
Otokoyama	Man Mountain
Momokawa	Peach River
Urakasumi	Mist of the Harbor
Harushika	Spring Deer
Kikusui	Chrysanthemum Water
Shichifukujin	Seven Gods of Good Fortune
Oyama	Big Mountain
Hatsumago	First Grandchild
Hitori Musume	Only Daughter
Kobai	Fragrant Plum
Yoakemae	Just Before Dusk
Kiyoizumi	Clean Spring
Buyu	Courage of the Warrior
Sato no Homare	Pride of the Village
Shinkame	Sacred Turtle
Isojiman	Pride of the Peninsula
Yamatsuru	Mountain Crane
Kokuryu	Black Dragon
Yorokobi no Izumi	Spring of Delight
Toyo no Aki	Autumn of Abundance
Suigei	Drunken Whale
Nishi no Seki	Western Gate
Hakutsuru	White Crane
Ozeki	Champion

Saké Cocktails

Purists, go ahead and cringe, but saké is wonderful in cocktails. In fact, because of its lower alcohol content compared with gin, vodka, or rum, saké is often the preferred mixer. Here are some of our favorite saké cocktail recipes.

SAKÉ MARTINI

Dry saké with a dash of dry vermouth. Served with a speared olive or slice of cucumber.

SAKÉ MARGARITA

Mix dry saké with Triple Sec and lime juice, then shake and pour over ice and serve in a glass with salt-coated rim and a lime wedge or slice of Japanese citron (*yuzu*).

BLOODY MARY WITH SAKÉ

Combine dry saké with tomato juice, Tabasco sauce, Worcestershire sauce, squeeze of lime, salt and pepper. Serve over ice with a celery stick.

PURPLE HAZE

Mix Chambord with dry saké and serve in a martini glass.

SAKÉ LATTE

Mix a Nigori or Nigori Genshu saké with coffee liqueur and serve on the rocks.

SAKÉ SLUSHY

Freeze a bottle of Genshu saké (at least three hours) and pour into a tumbler—the liquid saké turns into a saké slushy. This only works with Genshu saké, which is 20% alcohol.

FOODS TO TRY WITH SAKÉ: SAKANA

Foods eaten with saké are called *sakana*. Saké being made from rice, sakana dishes do not use rice in their preparation. The topic of food and saké could easily fill several books on its own, but here are a few of the more "interesting" *sakana* commonly enjoyed with saké in Japan.

- *Kanimiso*: Crab brains, the grayish stuff in the crustacean's head that no one eats in the U.S. Rich and tasty with saké.

- *Karasumi*: Dried, pressed, mullet roe. Very expensive and labor intensive to make. Rich and interesting flavor. Hard to top this.

- *Shiokara*: Salted fish innards. Some like 'em, some don't. Salty and a good palate cleanser.

- *Sashimi*: Raw fish of all varieties. Nothing weird about this, since most Americans are already familiar with sushi. Wine and cheese have nothing over the saké and sashimi combination.

Six Quick and Easy Dishes Using Saké

Cooking with saké opens up a whole new realm of flavor sensations. Anything that uses wine in cooking can use saké instead. The big argument among chefs is whether the quality of saké you use in cooking matters. Is a Ginjo saké better to use than an ordinary saké? Is it OK to use stale saké? Our conclusion is that the quality of saké used, particularly with flavor-sensitive, delicate foods like fresh seafood, does make a difference. With heartier foods, such as pork, you can use slightly stale saké without unpleasant results. (What to do with the really stale saké? Use it for bathing: one 750 ml bottle per large bath!) Here are some of our favorite simple recipes that use saké.

BROILED SALMON

Ingredients

filet of salmon or salmon steaks individually cut
into serving sizes
⅔ cup of saké (preferably fresh saké)
⅔ cup of soy sauce

Marinate the salmon in the saké and soy
sauce for about 15 minutes.

Broil each side in the oven for about 5
minutes or until slightly brown.

SHREDDED CHICKEN

Ingredients

chicken breasts
½ cup saké
½ cup water
1 tbsp soy sauce

Cut chicken breasts into strips

Bring saké, water, soy sauce to a boil in a
wok.

Add chicken strips while constantly turning
the chicken in the saké until cooked.

Remove and cool the chicken. Then shred
the chicken by hand for use in appetizers or
salads. Season to taste.

PORK APPETIZER

Ingredients

pork shoulder
3 cups saké
2 cups water
¼ cup soy sauce

1 cup dashi (powdered fish broth, available
from Asian food stores)
1 tbsp brown sugar
1 tbsp miso (soybean paste)
mustard or horseradish

Cut pork shoulder into 2-inch cubic pieces,
trim fat as desired.

Cook in oil in a skillet on high heat until
brown on all sides.

Place browned meat in another pot and
simmer in 2 cups of saké and 2 cups of water
for 90 minutes.

Pour liquid out; add additional 1 cup of
saké, soy sauce, dashi, brown sugar, and
miso to the pork. Simmer another 90 minutes with an inner lid (you can use a plate as
the inner lid) under the regular lid on the pot.

Makes a terrific appetizer with hot mustard
or horseradish throughout the week.

MUSHROOMS À LA SAKÉ

Ingredients

portobello, shiitake, and oyster mushrooms
½ cup saké
½ cup soy sauce
½ cup dashi (powdered fish broth, available
from Asian food stores)

Slice portobello mushrooms and quarter the
shiitake and oyster mushrooms.

Cook mushrooms together in a pan with ½
cup of saké, ½ cup soy sauce, and ½ cup of
dashi for about 7 minutes. Season to taste.

FRESH BERRIES WITH GOLDEN SAKÉ SAUCE

Ingredients

2 pints fresh berries (or other fresh fruit)
¼ cup Nigori or Nigori Genshu saké
1 cup sour cream
¼ cup brown sugar
1 tsp grated lemon peel

Rinse and drain berries and remove stems.

    Combine sour cream with brown sugar and lemon peel and mix until sugar is well blended. Add saké and mix.

    Place berries in individual bowls and divide sauce over fruit.

CONFETTI CLAMS

Ingredients

2½ pounds butter clams or other small clams in shells
½ cup saké
1½ cups water
3–4 tbsp olive oil
2 Anaheim peppers or 1 green pepper
1 yellow bell pepper
1 red bell pepper
½ cup onion, chopped
8 medium mushrooms
1 tsp ginger root, grated
1 tbsp mirin
1 tbsp soy sauce
salt and pepper (optional)

SAKÉ AND BATHING

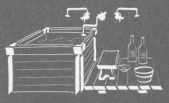

Putting saké into a hot bath and soaking your bones in some brew is said to be good for circulation and the skin. Known as a *sakaburo*, the highly civilized saké bath requires a half-liter to liter of saké for a good ten-minute soak. Any saké will do, but we do feel that you should probably use old bottles or unfinished bottles that have gone bad. Several saké brewers have from time to time marketed saké especially for use in the bath. Chances are it is not their top-of-the-line brew, but the drippings from a lower-grade pressing. By the way, and this is important, pour the saké into the bath, **NOT** into you. Mixing a hot Japanese bath and a state of inebriation is dangerous and can aggravate heart conditions or cause dizziness and fainting.

Let clams stand in cold, salted water for 1 hour. Scrub clams if dirty.

Rinse clams in clear water and place in heat-proof container that will fit inside a pan with a lid.

Pour ½ cup saké into clams container. Pour water into the pan (not into clams container). Bring water to boil, reduce heat, and simmer until clams open, approximately 5–10 minutes. As clams open, remove and place in a bowl. (Some clams may take longer to open then others. Be patient, but if a clam does not open within 15 minutes discard it.)

Cut peppers in half and remove seeds. Cut into small cubes or strips. Sauté peppers and onions in olive oil until tender but crisp. Do not overcook.

Wash and quarter mushrooms. Add garlic, mushrooms, and ginger root and sauté a few minutes longer. Remove from heat.

Pour liquid from clams container into vegetables. Add mirin, soy sauce, salt and pepper to taste, and clams. Stir together over medium heat 2-4 minutes or until warm. Serve in bowls as a main dish.

A JAZZY BREW

In our opinion, the juxtaposition of a Western-style jazz piano and Japanese-style instruments makes the ultimate saké-sipping music. Keiko and Kazu Matsui are a Japanese couple who are better known in the U.S. than in Japan. Keiko is a jazz pianist, while Kazu plays a large bamboo flute, called a shakuhachi, which produces a very Japanese sound. The Matsuis have released a number of CDs in the U.S. Turn down the lights, turn on the stereo, raise your glass, relax.

SAKÉ SIPPING WEAR

"Saké Pure + Simple" means saké just as it comes from the bottle, with no adornments or fancy ceremonies. You don't have to "dress up" saké, and you don't have to dress yourself up to drink it either. But if you really want to get into saké sartorial splendor, here are two suggestions. Try slipping into a *yukata*, a lightweight cotton kimono (often seen at bathhouses and hot springs resorts). There are lots of great designs, from geometric patterns to flowers to frightening warrior faces. Great footsy opportunities under the table, too! Or try an American variation of the *jinbei*, an outfit traditionally worn by Japanese laborers: a *yukata* top sits over American-style overalls. This "fusion fashion" is the perfect blend of East meets West comfort clothing and is perfect when you need to strike just the right saké attitude.

THE FUTURE OF SAKÉ

NEW FANS, NEW STYLES

New Developments in Saké

Among sakés being created in saké kura in the United States, we are beginning to see some interesting trends. The first encouraging trend is a greater variety of premium chilled sakés being offered in addition to the jug quality "hot sakés." A second trend is that packaging on U.S.-brewed saké is becoming more consumer friendly with "fresh-ness dates" and more information in English about saké showing up on the bottle labels. A third trend is the move toward introducing sakés that by traditional Japanese sakémaster standards are quite radi-cal, and undoubtedly a number of Japanese sakémasters are turning over in their graves! An example is SakéOne's Moonstone line of infused sakés with flavors such as Asian Pear, Roasted Hazelnut, and Black Raspberry.

Emerging Saké Styles

Preferences in saké have changed over the decades, much like prefer-ences in other beverages. Because saké was, until relatively recently, a bit rougher and simpler than it is now, for a long time these prefer-ences merely went from dry to sweet and back again.

These days, however, the trend is a bit different. Many people have come to prefer fragrant, fruity saké. Although too much of such a good thing is possible, many people do enjoy the Ginjo bouquet (the *ginjo-ka*) of a fine saké. Yet there are those saké experts in Japan who feel this type of saké is too winelike, and find the nose and lively fla-vor to be too obtrusive.

What will happen in the U.S. as more and more people come to appreciate saké and learn its intricacies? What will happen when Americans take up saké brewing on a larger scale and start to forge their own style and niche?

It is quite likely that saké styles will begin to change again, heading toward the bold and expressive. Stronger flavors, wilder fragrances. Although this type of saké may not be prized, or even be considered drinkable, by saké connoisseurs in Japan, Americans are not so tied to tradition. Wine and craft beer are two good examples of traditional alcoholic beverages that have evolved dramatically under recent American influence.

This will certainly take some time to come about. Saké brewing is complex and takes years and years to master. But count on the saké brewers of the future in the U.S.—and other countries—to make their mark in the long and storied history of saké.

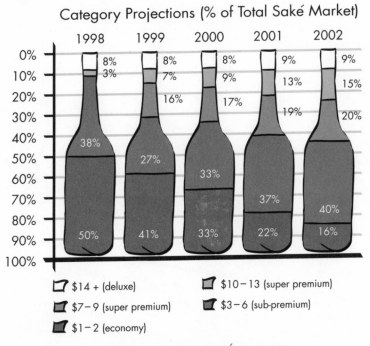

Category Projections (% of Total Saké Market)

	1998	1999	2000	2001	2002
$14 + (deluxe)	8%	8%	8%	9%	9%
$10–13 (super premium)	3%	7%	9%	13%	15%
$7–9 (super premium)		16%	17%	19%	20%
$3–6 (sub-premium)	38%	27%	33%	37%	40%
$1–2 (economy)	50%	41%	33%	22%	16%

◧ $14 + (deluxe)　　　　◧ $10–13 (super premium)

◧ $7–9 (super premium)　　◧ $3–6 (sub-premium)

◧ $1–2 (economy)

THE DEVELOPING SAKÉ MARKET

Over time, premium sakés, many of which are best drunk slightly chilled, will occupy more and more of the saké market, an indication of changing tastes, greater appreciation of saké's virtues, and a better-educated consumer.

RESOURCES

Books

Eckhardt, Fred. *Sake (U.S.A.): The Complete Guide to American Sake, Sake Breweries, and Homebrewed Sake.* Portland, OR: Fred Eckhardt Communications, 1992.

Gauntner, John. *The Saké Handbook.* Tokyo and Boston: Charles E. Tuttle, 1997.

Harper, Philip. *The Insider's Guide to Saké.* Tokyo and New York: Kodansha International, 1998.

Kondo, Hiroshi. *The Book of Saké.* Tokyo and New York: Kodansha International, 1996.

Web Sites

Internet addresses and sites change frequently. If the URLs provided here don't lead you to the site, try finding it through a search engine or keyword search. All hyphens in the URLs are a part of the address.

CHEMISTRY OF SAKÉ BREWING
http://hbd.org/brewery/library/chmsk_RA.html
This site provides the entire text of the book *The Chemistry of Saké Brewing*, written by R. W. Atkinson in 1881, in downloadable formats.

GEKKEIKAN SAKÉ
http://www.gekkeikan-sake.com/
The U.S. Gekkeikan brewery is located in Folsom, California, and its site includes product and tour information, as well as saké trend stories, a company history, and a link to its Japanese site.

HAKUSAN SAKÉ GARDENS
http://www.hakusan.com/
This well-designed site from the Napa, California, brewery includes information on its products, history, and distributors and has directions on how to visit.

HAKUSHIKA SAKÉ U.S.A.
http://www.sakeweb.com/
Hakushika is based in Colorado, and in addition to product information and saké news, the page includes information on the company staff and a contest.

HOW TO HOME-BREW SAKÉ
http://brewery.org/brewery/library/sake_MH0796.html
A quick and dirty, no-nonsense guide to homebrewing saké. Written by Mutsuo Hoshido.

AN INTRODUCTION
TO SAKÉ
http://www.lvdi.net/
~sringler/sake.html
This comprehensive
article includes an
excellent saké history
as well as information
on types, traditions,
homebrewing, recipes,
and other topics of
interest to saké lovers.

IZUMIBASHI
http://www.sphere.ad.
jp/izmibasi/
The homepage for this
Japanese saké brewery
contains the usual
information on mate-
rials, brewing, and
drinking saké, but has
the bonus of doing so
in fourteen different
languages.

THE JOY OF SAKÉ
http://www.
joyofsake.com/
This site provides a
nice tutorial on the
process of saké mak-
ing, from rice and
water to fermentation
and philosophy, as
well as a short history
of saké in America.

MICROSAKERY
http://www.
brewstore.com/sake_
page.html
Microbrewing comes
to saké. If you are
looking to distinguish
your restaurant (or if
you need ninety gal-
lons of saké at a time),
this may be the site for
you.

MOMOKAWA PREMI-
UM SAKÉ
http://www.
momokawa.com/
The site for this brew-
ery, located in Forest
Grove, Oregon,
includes product infor-
mation, a tour through
the brewery, recipes,
and distributor
information.

SAKÉ ASSOCIATION
OF AMERICA
http://www.sakeusa.
com/sake/index.html
This site for a consor-
tium of saké compa-
nies operating in the
U.S. provides descrip-
tions of the constit-
uent companies as
well as lots of general
saké information and a
variety of giveaways.

SAKÉ DIRECT
http://sake-direct.com/
If you live in the right
state, you can mail
order saké from the
comfort of your own
home. Saké Direct is a
retailer with a growing
selection of good
brews. The site also
includes reviews and
links to help those
who cannot receive
saké by mail order.

SAKÉ KINGDOM
http://manzoku.
topica.ne.jp/sake/
index_e.html
This small, high-ener-
gy site includes a saké
glossary, reports, and a
short article on saké's
role in the Japanese
end-of-the-year gift-
giving custom called
oseibo.

SAKÉ LABELS
http://ecbos.tmit.ac.jp/
sake/label.html
If you're tired of read-
ing, then try out this
site. No discussion, no
captions, just pictures
of saké labels upon
saké labels.

SAKÉ MERCHANDISE
http://www.
japanesegifts.com/
adishes.asp
If you don't want to
paper-bag your saké,
you may be interested
in this site that offers
Japanese saké sets,
cups, bottles, and
wooden saké cups for
sale.

SAKÉONE
http://www.sakeone.
com
The only American-
owned brewery in the
world has information
about how you can
become a shareholder
in the first publicly
traded saké brewery in
the world.

SAKÉ RESOURCE
CENTER
http://www.sakes.com
Website of the Interna-
tional Saké Institute's
Saké Resource Center.
A comprehensive
source of information
in English about saké.

SAKÉ WORLD
http://www.
sake-world.com
The companion web

site to the *Saké World*
newsletter—by coau-
thor of this book John
Gauntner—includes
information on saké
books, events, consult-
ing, a Top 100 picks,
web links, and more.
A great one-stop site if
you're short on time.

SUIHITSU
http://www.suihitsu.
co.jp/eng/
Suihitsu ("Drunken
Pen") is a Japanese
magazine "related to
saké and culture." The
site includes a good
general information
section, as well as
news, reviews, and the
entire back catalog of
their magazine (unfor-
tunately in Japanese
only).

SUN MASAMUNE
BREWERY
http://www.sun-
masamune.com.au
The site for Australia's
first saké brewery con-
tains the usual back-
ground on saké, in
addition to directions
and tourist informa-
tion (if you're going to
be in Penrith, N.S.W.,

any time soon). There
is also an automated
ordering form.

TAKARA SAKÉ USA
http://sanfrancisco.
sidewalk.com/link/
10238
Located on the Web
pages of a San Francis-
co tour guide, the
Takara site provides
information about and
directions to the
Takara Brewery in
Berkeley, California.

TAMANOHIKARI
SAKÉ
http://www.sake.com
This site for the Japa-
nese saké Tamano-
hikari, in addition to
general information
on history, and saké
production, includes
tutorials on tasting and
choosing sakés, as well
as a worldwide guide
to restaurants that
serve the company's
brand.

TASTING CHARTS

Use the following "parameter preference" charts to track your tasting observations about the sakés you sample. Designed by coauthor John Gauntner, the chart tracks the eight parameters of preference that are discussed ☞ on pages 87–92. The format of the chart is an evolutionary development of the dry/sweetness scale (measured as the Saké Meter Value, or SMV) that is conventionally used to describe a saké's overall tasting profile. But while the SMV is an absolute measure, the values on the charts here are largely subjective. And that's the point. Your saké selections should be determined by your own likes and dislikes, not by what the critics say. Tasting takes time, deliberation, and a clean palate. Keep a glass of water handy as you taste, and be sure to share your observations with your friends. You may photocopy more charts as needed.

Saké brand:		Type:	
Brewery:		Tasting date:	
FRAGRANCE	none • • • • • • • • • •	fragrant
IMPACT	quiet • • • • • • • • • •	explosive
SWEET/DRY	sweet • • • • • • • • • •	dry
ACIDITY	soft • • • • • • • • • •	puckering
PRESENCE	unassuming • • • • • • • • • •	full
COMPLEXITY	straightforward • • • • • • • • • •	complex
EARTHINESS	delicate • • • • • • • • • •	dank
TAIL	quickly vanishing • • • • • • • • • •	pervasive
Where tasted:		SMV:	
Tasting notes:			

Saké brand:		Type:	
Brewery:		Tasting date:	

FRAGRANCE	none	•	•	•	•	•	•	•	•	•	•	fragrant
IMPACT	quiet	•	•	•	•	•	•	•	•	•	•	explosive
SWEET/DRY	sweet	•	•	•	•	•	•	•	•	•	•	dry
ACIDITY	soft	•	•	•	•	•	•	•	•	•	•	puckering
PRESENCE	unassuming	•	•	•	•	•	•	•	•	•	•	full
COMPLEXITY	straightforward	•	•	•	•	•	•	•	•	•	•	complex
EARTHINESS	delicate	•	•	•	•	•	•	•	•	•	•	dank
TAIL	quickly vanishing	•	•	•	•	•	•	•	•	•	•	pervasive

Where tasted:		SMV:	
Tasting notes:			

Saké brand:		Type:	
Brewery:		Tasting date:	

FRAGRANCE	none	•	•	•	•	•	•	•	•	•	•	fragrant
IMPACT	quiet	•	•	•	•	•	•	•	•	•	•	explosive
SWEET/DRY	sweet	•	•	•	•	•	•	•	•	•	•	dry
ACIDITY	soft	•	•	•	•	•	•	•	•	•	•	puckering
PRESENCE	unassuming	•	•	•	•	•	•	•	•	•	•	full
COMPLEXITY	straightforward	•	•	•	•	•	•	•	•	•	•	complex
EARTHINESS	delicate	•	•	•	•	•	•	•	•	•	•	dank
TAIL	quickly vanishing	•	•	•	•	•	•	•	•	•	•	pervasive

Where tasted:		SMV:	
Tasting notes:			

| Saké brand: | | | | | | | | | | | Type: |
| Brewery: | | | | | | | | | | | Tasting date: |

FRAGRANCE	none	•	•	•	•	•	•	•	•	•	•	fragrant
IMPACT	quiet	•	•	•	•	•	•	•	•	•	•	explosive
SWEET/DRY	sweet	•	•	•	•	•	•	•	•	•	•	dry
ACIDITY	soft	•	•	•	•	•	•	•	•	•	•	puckering
PRESENCE	unassuming	•	•	•	•	•	•	•	•	•	•	full
COMPLEXITY	straightforward	•	•	•	•	•	•	•	•	•	•	complex
EARTHINESS	delicate	•	•	•	•	•	•	•	•	•	•	dank
TAIL	quickly vanishing	•	•	•	•	•	•	•	•	•	•	pervasive

| Where tasted: | | | | | | | | | | | SMV: |
| Tasting notes: | | | | | | | | | | | |

| Saké brand: | | | | | | | | | | | Type: |
| Brewery: | | | | | | | | | | | Tasting date: |

FRAGRANCE	none	•	•	•	•	•	•	•	•	•	•	fragrant
IMPACT	quiet	•	•	•	•	•	•	•	•	•	•	explosive
SWEET/DRY	sweet	•	•	•	•	•	•	•	•	•	•	dry
ACIDITY	soft	•	•	•	•	•	•	•	•	•	•	puckering
PRESENCE	unassuming	•	•	•	•	•	•	•	•	•	•	full
COMPLEXITY	straightforward	•	•	•	•	•	•	•	•	•	•	complex
EARTHINESS	delicate	•	•	•	•	•	•	•	•	•	•	dank
TAIL	quickly vanishing	•	•	•	•	•	•	•	•	•	•	pervasive

| Where tasted: | | | | | | | | | | | SMV: |
| Tasting notes: | | | | | | | | | | | |

Saké brand: Type:

Brewery: Tasting date:

FRAGRANCE	none · · · · · · · · · · ·	fragrant
IMPACT	quiet · · · · · · · · · · ·	explosive
SWEET/DRY	sweet · · · · · · · · · · ·	dry
ACIDITY	soft · · · · · · · · · · ·	puckering
PRESENCE	unassuming · · · · · · · · · · ·	full
COMPLEXITY	straightforward · · · · · · · · · · ·	complex
EARTHINESS	delicate · · · · · · · · · · ·	dank
TAIL	quickly vanishing · · · · · · · · · · ·	pervasive

Where tasted: SMV:

Tasting notes:

Saké brand: Type:

Brewery: Tasting date:

FRAGRANCE	none · · · · · · · · · · ·	fragrant
IMPACT	quiet · · · · · · · · · · ·	explosive
SWEET/DRY	sweet · · · · · · · · · · ·	dry
ACIDITY	soft · · · · · · · · · · ·	puckering
PRESENCE	unassuming · · · · · · · · · · ·	full
COMPLEXITY	straightforward · · · · · · · · · · ·	complex
EARTHINESS	delicate · · · · · · · · · · ·	dank
TAIL	quickly vanishing · · · · · · · · · · ·	pervasive

Where tasted: SMV:

Tasting notes:

INDEX

Thanks for all those saké moments to DB, GF, "Greg," Ven. Anzan Hoshin, JG, Marian Kinoshita, Michael McVey, Melissa Otto-Yano, PG, Jeff Sampson, Andrew W. Silberman, and many others who told us of some of the great times they now associate with saké. If you have a saké moment you'd like to share, send it to the Editor at sbp@stonebridge.com. Kanpai!